YOGA SASTRA:

THE YOGA SUTRAS OF PATANJALI EXAMINED;

WITH A NOTICE

OF

SWAMI VIVEKANANDA'S YOGA PHILOSOPHY

JOHN MURDOCH

GYAN

Published by

Gyan Publishing House
5, Ansari Road
Daryaganj, New Delhi-110002
Phone: 011-47034999, 9811692060
E-mail: books@gyanbooks.com

Distribution Network
gyanbooks.com
India, USA, Canada, UK, Australia

ISBN: 978-93-6780-248-9 (PB)

First Published, 1897

2nd Impression 2024

Printed at: Gyan Press, Delhi.

YOGA SASTRA
Author: JOHN MURDOCH

The Madras Brahman who claimed to sit in the air by Yoga powers.

REWARD OF Rs. 1,000.

The above sum is offered to any one who, by yoga powers, will raise himself three feet from the ground, and remain suspended for ten minutes. For conditions, see page 38.

The Sacred Books of the East Described and Examined.

YOGA SASTRA:

THE YOGA SUTRAS OF PATANJALI EXAMINED;

WITH A NOTICE

OF

SWAMI VIVEKANANDA'S YOGA PHILOSOPHY.

BARTH ON YOGA EXERCISES:

"Conscientiously observed, they can only issue in folly and idiocy."

Religions of India, p. 83.

"Ring out the old, ring in the new,
Ring out the false, ring in the true.

Tennyson.

FIRST EDITION, 3,000 COPIES.

THE CHRISTIAN LITERATURE SOCIETY FOR INDIA:

LONDON AND MADRAS.

1897.

PREFACE.

It has been the unhappy lot of India to have had for thousands of years a succession of teachers who palmed off their crude ideas as inspired. The result has been, in the words of Sir H. S. Maine, "false morality, false history, false philosophy, false physics."

All educated Hindus will admit that the history, geography, and astronomy of the Hindu sacred books are egregiously wrong. In the following pages it is shown that belief in Yoga powers and charms is equally mistaken. Marvellous power may indeed be acquired, but not by Yoga.

The reader is advised to follow the course pointed out at page 58.

"Awakened India," instead of adopting the Fowl or Tortoise Upset Posture, with his eye fixed on the tip of his nose and seeking "the suppression of the transformations of the thinking principle," should rather endeavour to have his muscles braced like those of Prince Ranjitsinhji, his faculties of observation cultivated like those of Professor Bose, his ability to weigh evidence developed like that of Dr. Bhandarkar. Instead of a dreamy pessimism, let there be active benevolence. Thus would India advance in civilization with a speed before unknown.

"Above all, let the deep religious feeling of the Hindu mind be wisely directed. Let the *Bhakti Yoga* have for its object the loftiest ideal of majesty, wisdom, goodness and purity. Such is the great Creator and Lord of the Universe."

J. MURDOCH.

CONTENTS.

YOGA SASTRA.

INTRODUCTION.

NATIONS, as well as individuals, have their peculiar dispositions. The English are fond of what is practical, bearing upon the concerns of life. Hence they have made great improvements in the arts; as railway travelling, steam navigation, &c. Hindus, on the contrary, have paid little attention to these things, but have shown a great inclination to discuss abstract philosophical questions or mystical religious speculations. There are six principal *Darsanas*, or schools of Hindu philosophy: viz.,

1. The *Nyáya*, founded by Gotama.
2. The *Vaiseshika*, by Kanáda.
3. The *Sánkhya*, by Kapila.
4. The *Yoga*, by Patanjali.
5. The *Mímánsá*, by Jaimini.
6. The *Vedánta* by Bádaráyana or Vyása.

An account of the whole is given in *Philosophic Hinduism*.* The Sánkhya system will first be briefly explained, as it is intimately connected with the Yoga.

THE SANKHYA SYSTEM.

As already stated, this is attributed to Kapila, a supposed irascible Rishi, who reduced to ashes the 60,000 sons of king Sagara. To attract attention, it was a common practice among Hindus to claim some renowned rishi as the author of a treatise.

The chief exponents of the system are the *Sánkhya Karika* and the *Sánkhya Pravachana*. The former has been translated into English by Mr. Davies; the latter by Dr. Ballantyne. The *Sánkhya Pravachaná* consists of six books and 526 sutras. The Sánkhya, says Mr. Manilal, "starts with the propositions that the world is full of miseries of three kinds, physical, (*ádhibhautika*) supernatural (*ádhidaivika*), and corporeal (*ádhyátmika*); and that those are the results of the properties of matter (*prakrti*), and not of its inseparable correlate of intelligence of consciousness (*purusa*)†

The grand object of the system is set forth in the 1st aphorism: "Well, the complete cessation of pain, (which is) of three kinds is the complete end of man."

---

* Sold by Mr. A. T. Scott, Tract Depôt, Madras, 8vo. 72 pp. 2½ As. Post-free, 3 As.

† *The Yoga Sutra of Patanjali*, p. iii.

The immediate cause of the bondage of the soul is the conjunction of *Prakriti* and the soul. The remedy is the liberation of the soul by knowledge.

According to the Sánkhya, there are two eternally existing entities, *Prakriti* and souls.

Prakriti denotes that which produces or brings forth every thing else. It is sometimes not very accurately rendered "Nature."* Monier Williams says, that "producer, originator, would more nearly express the meaning." From the absence of a root in the root, the root of all thing is rootless.

Prakriti is supposed to be made up of three principles, called *Gunas,* or cords, supposed to bind the soul. They are *Sattva, Rajas, Tamas*; or Truth, Passion, and Darkness. These principles enter into all things; and on the relative quantity of each in any object depends the quality of the object.

Souls (*Purush*) are countless in number; individual, sensitive, eternal, unchangeable. All that is done by Prakriti is done on behalf of soul. In its own nature soul is without qualities, until united with Prakriti. The union of the two is compared to a lame man mounted on a blind man's shoulders; the pair are then both (as it were) capable of perception and movement.

Beginning from the original rootless germ Prakriti, the Sánkhya counts up (*san-khyáti)* synthetically (whence its name of 'synthetic enumeration') twenty-three other Tattwas or entities—all productions of the first and evolving themselves spontaneously out of it, as cream out of milk, or milk out of a cow,—while it carefully distinguishes them all from a twenty-fifth, *Purusha,* the soul, which is wholly in its own nature destitute of Gunas, though liable to be bound by the Gunas of Prakriti.

According to the Sánkhya system, the five grosser elements (*mahábhúta*) with their distinguishing properties and corresponding organs of sense are the following:

	Distinguishing Property.	Organ of Sense.
1. *Akása,* ether	Sound	The Ear
2. *Váyu,* air,	Tangibility	The Skin
3. *Tejas,* fire, light,	Colour	The Eye
4. *Apas,* water,	Taste	The Tongue
5. *Prithiví,* earth	Smell	The Nose

There are eleven organs produced by *Ahankára,* the five organs of sense, ear, skin, eye, tongue, nose; and five organs of actions, largest (the throat), hand, foot, and excretory and generative organs, and an eleventh organ standing between them *viz., Manas,* 'the mind' which is regarded as an internal organ of perception, volition, and action.

The liberation of *Purusha,* or soul, from the fetters which

---

* Mr. Manilal translates it "Matter" p. iii.

bind it in consequence of its union with Prakriti is done by conveying the correct knowledge of the 24 constituent principles of creation, and rightly discriminating the soul from them.*

Mr. Manilal says: "The inseparable *prakriti* and *purusha* are enough in themselves to account for the whole of the phenomena of the universe, and the idea of a Creator is looked upon by the Sánkhyas as a mere redundant phantom of philosophy." It is therefore known among Hindus by the name of *Nirisvara Sánkhya*, or the *Sánkhya without Isvara*.

The Yoga is commonly regarded as a branch of the Sánkhya; but as it nominally acknowledges the existence of God, it is called *Sesvara Sánkhya, Sánkhya with Isvara*. Such was the popularity of the Sánkhya and Yoga, that the Mahábhárata, Sántiparvam, says: "There is no knowledge equal to the Sánkhya, and no power equal to the Yoga."

Before describing the Yoga system, an important question will first be considered.

THE GREAT AIM OF HINDU PHILOSOPHY.

The hymns of the Rig Veda take a cheerful view of life. The early Aryans had come from a cold bracing climate, encouraging labour. The doctrine of transmigration was then unknown. The usual petitions in the Rig Veda are for long life, sons, and abundance of cows. "The good went at death to the happy abode of Yama, and as *pitris* became quasi divinities themselves."

After the Aryans had settled in India for some time, they began to feel the influence of the hot, enervating climate. Labour was a burden; undisturbed repose seemed the highest bliss. A belief in transmigration also arose, and swayed the minds of the Hindus with tremendous power. The series of births is virtually endless; the common statement is that it rises to 84 lakhs. According to the merit or demerit of a human being, he is born afresh into the body of a man, or a beast, or a bird, or a fish, or a plant or a stone. "Ah this fearful round of births!" said the Marathi poet Tukaram, "this weary coming and going; when will it all end?' "With the Upanishads commences that great wail of sorrow which, for countless ages, has in India been rising up to heaven." It was intensified by Buddha. The first of the "four noble truth," which he professed to have discovered is, that "Existence is suffering." As a devout Buddhist counts his beads, he mutters *Anitya, Dukha, Anatta*, "Transience, Sorrow, Unreality." In the Vishnu Purana Book VI. Chapter 5, the evils of existence are described. It may be thus very briefly summarised:

---

* Abridged from *Hinduism*, by Monier Williams, S.P.C.K. 2*s*. 6*d*.

Bodily pain is of many kinds; as fever, spleen, dysentery, leprosy. Mental sufferings are anger, fear, hate, jealousy, envy, and many other passions. Affliction is multiplied in thousands of shapes in the progress of conception, birth, decay, disease, death, and hell. But not in hell alone do the souls of the deceased undergo pain; there is no cessation even in heaven; for its temporary inhabitant is ever tormented with the prospect of descending again to earth. Again is he liable to conception, birth, youth, manhood, old age, and death.

The body is described as a filthy receptacle of worms. The grand inquiry therefore is, how to "cut short the eighty-four," how to get rid of the curse of existence? *Mukti,* liberation from future births, is the grand aim of Hindu philosophy. Different means are prescribed for the attainment of *Mukti;* but remarks will here be confined to those enjoined by the Yoga.

YOGA SASTRA.

Founder.—The Yoga system is attributed to Patanjali.. Very little is known of some of the greatest Indian philosophers and authors. There is a very learned commentary, called the *Mahábháshya* on the Grammar of Pánini, by an author called Patanjali; but though the names are the same, they were probably different men. Of the former nothing is known. Patanjali describes the system, of which he may be merely the compiler, in 195 sutras; divided into four Books. Like most other sutras, they are obscure, and require commentaries.

Objects.—The word *Yoga* now usually means *union*: and it is generally understood to teach how the human soul may attain complete union with the Supreme Soul. But Patanjali gives it a different meaning:

"*Yoga* is the suppression of the transformations of the thinking principle." I. 2.*

Monier Williams interprets this as the "act of fixing or concentrating the mind in abstract meditation, and this is said to be effected by preventing the modifications of the thinking principle."†

Mr. R. C. Bose thus explains what is meant by the "transformations of the thinking principle:"

"One of the universally admitted maxims of Hindu philosophy is that the mind assumes the form of which it perceives; and therefore it necessarily becomes, really not figuratively, a tree, a tank, an animal, a sweet mango, a musical pipe, an odoriferous flower, or a hard stone: Not only so, it is changed into the grotesque forms and shapes conjured

---

* Translation by Manilal Nabhubhai Dvividi, p. 1.

† *Indian Wisdom*, pp. 92, 93.

up by fancy either when we are awake or when we are asleep, or into the ideas, equally subjective, exhumed by memory from the vaults of its own mausoleum. Who can form an adequate idea of its volability its fickleness, its restlessness? Who can number the varieties of mutations and transformations through which it passes in the course of the day, not to say a year, a decade, or the course of a long life? To destroy this fickleness, this changeableness, this restlessness, to lead the mind to wade, so to speak, through these innumerable transformations to its original state of serene repose—such is the object proposed by the Yoga Philosophy. The idea of union with God is a later graft.*

Mr. Manilal, thus explains this "transformation:"

"Knowledge or perception is a kind of transformation (*parináma*) of the thinking principle into anything which is the subject of external or internal presentation. All knowledge is of the kind of transformations of the thinking principle. Even the Will, which is the very first essential of *Yoga*, is a kind of such transformation. *Yoga* is a complete suppression of the tendency of the thinking principle to transform itself into objects, thoughts, &c."†

Hindus generally regard Yoga chiefly as the means by which occult powers are considered to be attainable. They are thus described by the Rev. Krishna Mohun Banerjea:

"By abstracting the corporeal senses from their ordinary media of communication, the Yoga is endowed with *heavenly* senses. He may not see or hear what passes around,—he may be insensible to external impressions,—but he has intuitions of things which his neighbours cannot see or hear. He becomes so buoyant, or rather so *sublimated* by his Yoga, that gravitation, or as Bháskarácbárya calls it, *the attractive power of the earth,* has no influence over him. He can walk and ascend in the sky, as if he were suspended under a balloon. He can, by this intuitive process, inform himself of the mysteries of astronomy and anatomy—of all things in fact that may be found in any of the different worlds. He may call to recollection the events of a previous life. He may attain an insight into the past and future. He may discern the thoughts of others, himself vanish at pleasure, and if he chose to do so, enter into his neighbour's body, and thus take possession of his living skin."‡

When Madame Blavatsky came to India, she claimed to possess some of these Yoga powers. She is said to have discovered a lost lady's ornament, to have created a cup and saucer, to have doubled a ring, to have repaired a broken China tray, to know what happened in distant places, to send letters through the air to Tibet, &c. In the hope of acquiring such occult powers, many Hindus paid an initiation fee of ten rupees. In time it was discovered that Madame Blavatsky's pretended wonders were mere juggler's tricks.

---

* *Hindu Philosophy*, p. 169.
† *The Yoga Sastra of Patanjali*, p. 2.
‡ *Dialogues on Hindu Philosophy*, pp. 69, 70.

The occult powers supposed to be acquired by Yoga will be more fully described hereafter.

At present also only the means to be employed for the suppression of the transformations of the thinking principle will be discussed.

Vritti (*Transformations*).

The act of the mind taking the shape of objects presented to it is called *vritti,* transformations. It is thus explained by Patanjali :

"The transformations are fivefold, and they are either painful or not painful. (They are) Right notions, misconception, fancy, sleep, and memory. Right notions are perception, inference, testimony. Misconception is incorrect notion, or a notion which abides in a form which is not that of its object. Fancy is a notion founded on knowledge conveyed by words, but of which there is no object corresponding in reality. Sleep is that transformation of the thinking principle which has for its object the conception of nothing. Memory is the not letting go of an object that has been recognised." Book I. 5-11.*

These five transformations of the thinking principle are the sources of its changeableness. Right notions of the objects around us are obtained, according to the Sánkhya School, by perception, inference, and testimony. Misconception or wrong notion arises from error, as when we mistake a rope for serpent. Fancy, *vikalpa,* is a notion to which there is nothing corresponding in nature, as the horns of a hare. In a sleep we have often dreams. Memory recalls past impressions, producing restlessness.

The Suppression of Transformations.

Sutra 12, Book I. says that the suppression of the transformations of the mind (*samádhi*) is to be secured by exercise and non-attachment (*vairágya.*)

Exercise is the steady effort to attain that state in which the mind stands unmoved, like the flame of a lamp in a place not exposed to the wind. *Rága,* attachment, is that which attracts the mind, and makes it assume different forms, as passions, sensations, &c.; *vairágya* is the absence of all attachment.

Iswara.

Iswara is thus defined by Patanjali :

"Iswara is a particular soul, which is untouched by affliction, works, deserts, and desires. In him the seed of the omniscient attains infinity. Being not limited by time, he is the greatest of the great. His indicator is the Pranava, Om, the word of glory." Book I. 24—27.

---

* Translation of Mr. Manilal and Dr. R. Mitra.

On account of the odium incurred by the Sánkhya system from its non-recognition of Iswara, Patanjali added him to the 25 elements of Kapila. Mr. R. C. Bose says:

"The entity brought in to satisfy a popular clamour or to humour current superstition, is as thoroughly a nonentity as the soul is. God, like the soul, is perfectly quiescent, and inactive. He does not create, does not preserve, does not destroy—these important functions being all discharged by Prakriti, the active principle which exists independently of him, and over the evolutions of which He has only a nominal rather than a real control.

"The being called Isvara posited by the Yoga school, is a nonentity rather than an entity, devoid of moral qualities as well as of natural properties, and devoid therefore of all those phenomena by which alone existence can manifest itself." pp. 163, 164.

Repetition of Om.

In Sutra 27, Om is called the "word of glory." The next Sutra says: "Its constant repetition (*japa*) and intent meditation on its meaning (should be practised)." Book I.

Mr. Manilal says: "All sacred books, from the Veda to the Purana, teach that this mystic syllable is the secret of secrets, and the source of all power."* It is thus explained in the Mundaka Upanishad:

"The sacred word (Om) is called the bow, the arrow the soul, and Brahma its aim; he shall be pierced by him whose attention does not swerve. Then he will be of the same nature with him (Brahma), as the arrow (becomes one with the aim when it has pierced it)." II. 4.

The repetition should be accompanied by meditation on the meaning.

"Obstacles" to Progress.

These are enumerated as follows:

"Disease, languor, doubt, carelessness, idleness, worldly-mindedness, mistaken notions, missing the point, and instability; these, causing distractions, are the obstacles." Book I. 33.

Doubt refers to the usefulness of meditation. Worldly mindedness denotes attachment to the things of the world. Mistaken notions are illustrated by mistaking mother-of-pearl for silver. Missing the point is going astray from the real point, *Samádhi*. Those things distract the mind, and are hindrances to Yoga.

The next Sutra states that "Pain, distress, trembling, inspiration and expiration, are the accompaniments of the causes of distraction."

---

* *Yoga Sutra of Patanjali*. p. 17.

Our Feelings towards Others.

Sutra xxxiii, says:

"The mind (becomes) even by the practice of sympathy, compassion, complacency, and indifference, respectively towards happiness, misery, virtue, and vice." Book I.

The feelings are those most favourable to *yoga*. Sympathy is a fellow-feeling with others, rejoicing with the happy, and compassionating the miserable. At the sight of virtue, we should be pleased; but for vice indifference is the best attitude for one who aims at *Samádhi*, (Mr. Manilal.)

BOOK II.

Kriyayoga.

Kriyáyoga, or Preliminary *Yoga*, denotes the exercises which are useful as preparatory to Samádhi. They are thus stated:

"Kriyáyoga (consists of) mortification, study, and meditation on Isvara. (They are practised) for acquiring habitual *Samádhi* and for lessening distractions." Book II. 1, 2.

Mortification denotes fasts, penances, &c.; Study, the repetition of *Om* &c. or the reading of religious books. The distractions whose causes should be lessened are mentioned in the next Sutra.

The Five "Distractions."

Sutra 3 says:

Ignorance, egoism, desire, aversion, and attachment are the five distractions. Book II.

All distraction is misery. Dr. R. Mitra renders "distractions" by "afflictions." The grand cause is *ignorance*.

Ignorance is the source of those that follow, whether they be dormant, weak, intercepted or simple. II. 4.

Ignorance (*avidyá*) is thus defined:

Ignorance is taking the non-eternal, impure, painful, and non-soul, to be eternal, pure, joyous, and soul. II. 5.

It is thus explained by Mr. R. C. Bose:

'Ignorance is according to this, as to every other system of Hindu Philosophy, the ultimate cause of that bondage from which deliverance is to be ardently desired. Ignorance of what? Not of God and His attributes; nor of the teaching in His revelation; but of the essential and everlasting difference between soul and non-soul. The characteristics of the soul are in marked antitheses to the properties and qualities of matter and its evolutes. The soul is eternal, pure, and joyous; while matter, in at least its present forms, is non-eternal, impure, and painful. But we are labouring under the hallucination that the soul is impure and miserable, while the fact is that impurity and pain belong to matter, and cannot possibly appertain to soul. And the consequence of this ignorance is that we wish to see the connection of the pure spirit with impure and painful matter, perpetuated rather than dissolved." p. 171.

According to the Vedanta, ignorance denotes ignorance of the "great sentence," *Tat twam asi*, "It thou art."

Egoism is thus defined:

"Egoism is the identifying of the power that sees with the power of seeing. II. 6.

Ahankára, is rendered *egoism* by Dr. Mitra. Egoism comes from *ego*, I. Mr. Manilal translate it "the sense of being." "Self-consciousness" is another rendering. Mr. R. C. Bose says:

"Ignorance begets egoism, by which the seer is identified with the seeing faculty, the enjoyer is confounded with the instrument of enjoyment, and the soul is declared to be nothing more or less than one of its own material organs." p. 171.

The other "distractions" are thus explained:

"Desire (*rága*) is dwelling on pleasure. Aversion (*dvesa*) is dwelling on pain. Attachment (*abhinivesa*) is the strong desire for life seen even in the wise and sustained by its own force." II. 1—9.

Mr. R. C. Bose says:

"From egoism proceed a longing for pleasure, and a recoil from pain; and these instincts give birth to tenacity of life, or an aversion to that dissolution of the soul with the material organs on which true emancipation hinges." p. 172.

Mr. Manilal says:

"Desire for life is indeed the cause of attachment of every description, and the real cause at the bottom of every misery of which the world is full." p. 32.

Instead of "the desire for life" being the cause of all the misery in the world, it is a wise instinct implanted by the Creator in every living being for its preservation. Without it, the world would soon be a lifeless void. It is the desire of life, which makes people work to obtain food, or the sick to take medicine for a cure.

Distractions the Cause of Misery.

Sutras 12-14 are as follows:

"The results of works have their root in distractions, and are felt either in this manifested birth or in the unmanifested one. The root existing, the deserts are class (játi), age, and experience. They have joy or suffering for their fruit according as their cause is virtue or vice." Book II.

Distractions are said to be the cause of misery; for all *karmas* arise from them, and lead to happiness or misery. The results of *karma* are felt either in this life or some other incarnation. The fruits determine our position in society, the length or shortness of our life, the pleasantness or the reverse of our experiences.

"All is Misery to the Discriminating."

Sutra 15 says:

"To the discriminating *all* is *misery*, on account of the opposition of the actions of the three qualities, and on account of consequences, anxiety, and impressions." Book II.

"The discriminating" are those who have made some progress in *yoga*, and are able to distinguish between what really exists and the illusive. To them every existence is not only full of misery, but misery itself. For this four reasons are assigned. The struggle between the three *gunas* must lead to disorder and misery. Pleasure is always followed by pain. It is also accompanied by anxiety. Every experience leaves an impression which creates a desire for enjoyment, leading in the end to misery.

According to the Hindu pessimistic dogma, "existence is suffering" and the sooner it is extinguished the better. The Christian doctrine is that, *rightly employed*, "existence is happiness."

THE EIGHT ACCESSORIES OF YOGA.

Sutras 28, 29 are as follows:

"On the decay of impurity through the practice of the accessories of *yoga*, there is illumination of the understanding till discriminative knowledge results.

"Restraint (*yama*), obligation (*niyama*), posture (*ásana*), regulation of the breath, (*pránáyáma*), abstraction (*pratyáhára*), devotion, (*dháraná*) contemplation (*dhyána*), and *samádhi* are the eight accessories of yoga." II.

Mr. Manilal says that Sutra 28 points out the way to the enlightenment leading to discrimination, by the destruction of impurity, *i.e.*, causes of distraction.

Mr. R. C. Bose remarks:

"These eight means of Yoga are called its members as well as its accessories. The first five the outer, and the last three the inner members; and they indicate the varied stages, incipient as well as advanced, of that laborious and painful exercise which terminates in the extinction of the thinking principle. It being necessary to draw particular attention to them, they are set forth one after another, in the order in which they appear in the above extracts, with elucidating comments." pp. 175, 176.

1. YAMA (*Restraint*).

Sutra 30 says :

" Yama includes abstinence from slaughter, falsehood, theft, incontinence, and avarice." II.

It is thus explained by Mr. R. C. Bose :

" Restraint is the first step in all schemes of reformation, meaning as it does, abstinence from gross sins and sinful dispositions. The word slaughter (*himsá*) as used in the aphorism bearing upon it has a twofold meaning. It means religious sacrifices well as murder. The Yogi Philosophy is as thoroughly opposed to the doctrine of sacrifice as Buddhism; and it brings forward *veracity* as a substitute for the bloody rites, enjoined in the Vedas, while it promises 'jewels from all sides,' to him 'who is confirmed in abstinence from theft,' and represents attainment of vigour as inseparably connected with 'continence." It prohibits avarice not only in the sense in which the word is ordinarily used, but in a sense unknown perhaps to all but students of Hindu Philosophy. The avaricious longing for fresh bodies and fresh births, of which we are supposed to be conscious, is condemned as well as cupidity in the ordinary sense of the term. The first step of Yoga is renunciation of sin in act, word, and even thought. So far it is worthy of commendation." p. 176.

Mr. Manilal, in his commentary, also considers that the restraint refers to thoughts as well as outward acts. *Himsá* prohibits the wishing evil to any being; continence forbids lustful thoughts. The restraint of such is far more difficult than of outward acts.

2. NIYAMA (*Obligation.*)

Sutra 32 says :

" The obligations are purity, contentment, penance, study, and devotion to Isvara." II.

Mr. Manilal remarks : "The duties hitherto described are negative or of the kind of omission ; those enjoined here are positive or of commission."

The effect of " Study" is thus defined :

" By study (is produced) communion with the desired deity." II. 44.

Mr. Manilal explains it as " the constant, silent, and devoted repetition of certain formulæ." page 49.

Mr. R. C. Bose thus comments on the Sutra :

" The second step is the cultivation of right dispositions within us by strict conformity to the commandments and ordinances of religion. A careful study of the Vedas, certain prescribed austerities and devotion to the Lord, are fitted to purify the soul from all its base desires, and breed contentment in it. There would be no objection to this statement, if by 'devotion to Isvara' were meant something more than muttering mechanically the two words *Pranava* and *Om*, which are represented as his symbols. It is affirmed that the frequent repetition of these symbols, or of some select verses from the Vedas, such as the Gayatri, leads to God-vision. Through muttering results *vision*, as explained by Bhoj Raja, of the desiderated deity. But God-vision according to this philosophy is tantamount to nothing-vision—the God posited being a nonentity!" pp. 176, 177.

3. Asana (*Posture*).

The third accessory is thus explained:

"Posture is that which is firm and pleasant. By mild effort and meditation on the endless. Then no assaults from the pairs of opposites." II. 46-48.

Mr. R. C. Bose says that "Vasistha, Yajnavalkya, and other sages of the Vedic and post-Vedic age fixed the number of postures at 84, stating that these had been prescribed and described by Siva, the father of Indian Yogis. Gorakshínátha, a Yogi of a later date, disgusted with their paucity, swelled their number to 84 lakhs." p. 177.

Dr. R. L. Mitra makes the following introductory remarks, quoted by Mr. Bose:

"Treating of a system of philosophy, Patanjala has not thought proper to enter into details regarding age, sex, caste, food, dwelling, etc., as bearing upon Yoga; but other works supply information about them to a considerable extent. A few notes derived therefrom may not be unfitly added here. The first question that would arise would be, Who are fit to perform the Yoga? On this subject the *Hatha Dipiká* fixes no limit. It says, 'By the practice of Yoga, every one may attain perfection, whether he be youthful, or old or very old, or diseased or decrepid.' The next point in the selection of a proper place. 'A small monastery, a dwelling not larger than a cube of six feet, situated in a out-of-the-way place, where there is no danger, within a circuit of a bow, of hail, fire, and water, in a country abounding in food, and free from danger of wars and the like, where religion prevails in a thriving kingdom,' is the most appropriate. The cell, or *mathika*, should have a small door, and no window; it should be free from holes, cavities, inequalities, high steps, and low descents. It should be smeared with cow-dung, not infested by vermin, with a terrace in front, a good well, and the whole surrounded by a wall. Dwelling in such a place, avoiding all anxieties, the Yogi should follow the path pointed out by his teachers in the exercise of the Yoga. He should avoid all excess of food, violent exertions, and vain disputations. His food should consist of wheat, sáli rice, barley, shasti rice (or that which matures in six days), the *syama* and the *nivára* grains, milk, clarified butter, coarse or candied sugar, butter, honey, ginger, palval, fruits, five kind of greens, mung pulse, and water, and all soothing sweet things in a moderate quantity, avoiding flesh-meat and too much salt, acids, and all stale putrid, decomposed, or acrid substances. The quantity of food taken should be such as to leave one-fourth of his appetite unappeased." p. 110.

Asana (*Postures.*)

Of the 84 postures ten are considered as the more important. The following are some of them as translated by Dr. R. L. Mitra:

"*Padmásana.* The right foot should be placed on the left thigh, and the left foot on the right thigh; the hands should be crossed, and the two great toes should be firmly held thereby; the chin should be bent down on the chest; and on this posture the eyes should be directed to the tip of the nose. It is called Padmásana (lotus-posture), and is highly beneficial in overcoming all diseases.

"*Gomukha.* Put the right ankle on the left side of the chest, and similarly, the left ankle on the right side, and the posture will be Gomukha, or the shape of a cow's mouth.

"*Fowl Posture.* Having established the lotus-posture, if the hand be passed between the thigh and the knees, and placed over the earth so as to raise the body aloft, it will produce the fowl-seat.

"*The Tortoise Upset Posture.* Having assumed the fowl posture, should the two hands be placed on the sides of the neck, it will make the posture like that of the tortoise upset; it is called tortoise upset posture.

"*Bow Posture.* Hold the great toes with the hands, and draw them to the ears as in drawing a bowstring, and this is called the bow posture." p. 104.

Mr. Manilal quotes the following additional postures from the *Hathapradipiká*:

"*Svastikásana.* Sit with the body perfectly straight after placing the right foot in the cavity between the left thigh and the calf, and the left foot in the cavity between the right thigh and the calf.

"*Siddhásana.* Having pressed the perinæum with the end of the left foot, place the right foot on the spot exactly above the penis. Then fix the chin steadily on the heart, and remaining unmoved like a post, direct the eyes to the spot in the middle of the brows." Appendix, p. ii.

Benefits of Posturing.—Sutra 48 says, "There no assaults from the pairs of opposites." Mr. Manilal explains this as follows:

"The pairs of opposites are heat and cold, pleasure and pain, love and sorrow, &c., constituting the whole of our worldly experience. When one proper posture is fully mastered, effects of the 'pairs of opposites' are not at all felt. It is necessary to obtain such mastery over any one posture before proceeding further." p. 51.

4. Pranayama. (*Regulation of the Breath.*)

Pránáyáma, is an important part of Yoga. The process consists of inspiration, expiration, and retention of the breath according to fixed rules. Patanjali's three Sutras on the subject are thus translated by Mr. Manilal:

"The (posturing) being (accomplished), *pránáyáma* (follows,—the cutting off of the course of inspiration and expiration (of the breath). (It is) external, internal or steady; regulated by place, time, and number; and is long or short. The fourth is that which has reference to the internal and external subject." II. 49-51.

The expiration of the breath is called *rechaka;* its inspiration *puraka;* its suspension *kumbhaka.* Mr. Manilal, says:

"*Pránáyáma*, has as its chief object the mixing of *prána*, the upper breath, and *apána*, the lower breath, and raising them upwards, by degrees and stages, till they subside in the head. The practice awakens a peculiar force which is dormant about the navel, and is called *Kundalini.* It is this force which is the source of all occult powers." p. 52.

Mr. Manilal quotes the following directions from the *Hatha-pradipiká*:

"So long as the *Nádis*, the vehicles of *prána*, are obstructed by abnormal humours, there is no possibility of the *prána* running in the middle course (*sasumná*) and of accomplishing the *unmami mudra.* Hence pránáyáma should be practised, in the first instance, for the clearance of these humours. The *pránáyáma* for this purpose is as follows. Having assumed the *padmásana* posture, the *yogin* should inhale at the left nostril, and having retained the breath for a time he easily can, should let it off at the opposite nostril; and repeat the same process beginning with the nostril where he exhales. This will make one *pránáyáma.* These should be practised 4 times in 24 hours, in the morning, at noon, in the evening at midnight, and should be slowly carried to 80 each time." Appendix, pp. iii, iv.

Other exercises are mentioned:

"*Uddiyána* consists in drawing in the navel and the parts above and below it. *Mulabandha* consists is drawing in the parts of the anus, and in mentally exerting as if to draw the *apána* upward towards the navel. The *jálandhara* consists in pressing the chin to the heart." III. 58, 27. Appendix v.

Dr. R. L. Mitra says:

"The time devoted to inspiration is the shortest, and to retention the longest. A Vaishnava in his ordinary daily prayer repeats the Vij-mantra (containing specific mystic syllables) once when expiring, seven times while inspiring, and twenty times when retaining. A Shakta repeats the mantra 16 times while inspiring, 64 times while retaining, and 32 times while expiring. These periods are frequently modified. As a rule it may be said that the longer the retention, the more proficient is the Yogi.*"

Pránáyáma will be further noticed under another head.

5. PRATYAHARA *(Abstraction)*.

Mr. Manilal thus translate the Sutra in which this is explained:

"Abstraction is, as it were, the imitating by the senses, the thinking principle, by withdrawing themselves from their objects." II. 54.

* Quoted by Mr. R. C. Bose, pp. 179, 180.

Mr. R. C. Bose has the following remarks on this means:

"Abstraction of the senses is effected by their withdrawal from the objects toward which they are attracted almost irresistibly, and by their concentration on the thinking principle. The senses cannot be extinguished so long as the body of which they are inseparable organs continues; but their natural tendency may not merely be counteracted but completely neutralized. Their natural tendency is to go outward toward the varieties of tempting objects in which the world abounds; and where they have their full play unrestrained, they prove sources of ceaseless change to the mind, and through it to the other internal organs and the soul. Their natural action must therefore be, not only restrained and circumscribed, but completely paralyzed or rather annihilated, and an action to which they are naturally averse substituted in its place. The mind must draw them in as a tortoise withdraw its limbs within its shell; and when thus fixed upon the soul itself they cease to be sources of restlessness and trouble." pp. 180, 181.

BOOK III.

6. DHARANA (*Devotion*).

Sutra 1, says:

"*Dháraná* is the fixing of the mind on something." III.

It is thus explained by Mr. R. C. Bose:

"The sixth step in this exercise is the confinement of the thinking principle to one place. In the earlier stages of meditation, the mind is not fitted for concentration on its great theme of contemplation, *viz.*, the soul. It must therefore be fixed on an external object, either through the eye, or without the help of any of the senses. That external object may be the tip of the nose, or the navel-wheel, or a plexus (net-work) of nerves in the belly, or the crown of the head or the sky or ether. When the thinking principle has acquired by such exercise the power of concentration, it may easily be transformed from an external to an internal object, from the objective non-self to the subjective-self." pp. 181, 182.

7. DHYANA (*Contemplation*).

Mr. Manilal thus translates Sutra 2:

"The unity of the mind with it is absorption (Dhyána)." III.

He thus explains it:

"Absorption or *dhyána* is the entire fixing of the mind on the object thought of, to the extent of making it one with it. In fact the mind should, at the time, be conscious only of itself and the object." p. 54.

The comment of Mr. R. C. Bose is as follows:—

"*Dhyána*, or contemplation, is the concentration of the thinking principle, not on an external object like the tip of the nose or the crown of the head, but on its proper object of thought. *Dhyána* is not the finishing stroke of the Yoga, because it is not accompanied with the obliteration of all distinction between the thinking principle, the object of thought, and thought itself. The state of perfect unconsciousness, which is the goal before the Yogi, is only a step ahead." p. 182.

8. Samadhi. (*Trance*).

A trance is a state in which the soul seems to have passed out of the body into another state of being; a state of insensibility to the things of this world. Mr. Manilal thus translates Sutra 3 defining it:

The same, when conscious only of the object, as if unconscious of itself, is trance." III.

He thus explains it:

" *Dhyána* carried to the extent of forgetting the act, and of becoming the thing thought of, is trance or *Samádhi.*" p. 55.

Mr. R. C. Bose says:

" *Samadhi*, or concentration, is the final stage in which the thinking principle loses its separate identity and becomes merged in the object of thought and thought itself; or rather in which the thinking principle is extinguished along with thought, and the object of thought remains in its original state of solitude. This state is called, *kaivalya*, translated 'abstraction' by Mr. Davies, 'isolation' by Dr. Mitra." p. 182.

Samayama.

Sutra 4 says:

"The three together constitute Samyama." III.

The three denote *Dháraná, dhyána,* and *samádhi*: *samyama* denotes them taken collectively. When the three are successively practised with respect to the same object at any one time, it is called *Samyama*.

Occult Powers resulting from Samyama.

Patanjali describes in different Sutras the wonderful powers which may be acquired through Samyama. They will be noticed in turn.

1. Knowledge of the past and future.

Sutra 16 says:

"The knowledge of past and future by *Samyama* on the three transformations." III.

Many important questions now involved in obscurity might thus be decided.

2. A Knowledge of the Sounds uttered by any being.

Two translations are given of Sutra 17 :

Dr. Mitra renders it :

"A confused comprehension of word, meaning, and knowledge arises from indiscriminate understanding. By *Samyama* with due discrimination is acquired an understanding of the cry of all creatures."

Mr. Manilal translates it :

"The word, its sense and knowledge, are confused with one another on account of their being mutually mistaken for one another ; hence by *Samyama* on the proper province of each, (arises) the comprehension of (the meaning) sounds uttered by any being."

The eternity of sound is a dogma of Hindu philosophy. Mr. Manilal offers the following explanation of the Sutra :

"Every meaning is eternally existent, and is as eternally connected with particular sounds, and therefore conveys or *reveals* the same sense wherever it is uttered. For letters are but the vehicles of the different sounds arising from the eight places within the body, *viz.*, the chest, the larynx, the root of the tongue, the teeth, the lips, the palate, the nose, and the head. Hence the divisions, &c. of letters. Therefore by performing *Samyama* on the three separately, the Yogin can comprehend the sense of all sounds uttered by any sentient being in nature. Even so can the music of nature be heard ; and the joyous *náda* within be cognised and understood." p. 63.

3. A Knowledge of former Births.

Sutra 18 is thus translated by Mr. Manilal :

"By mental presentation of the impressions a knowledge of former class." III.

Dr. Mitra renders it :

"A knowledge of former existence by making the residua (remains) apparent."

4. A Knowledge of the Minds of others.

Dr. Mitra, thus translates Sutra 19 :

"With reference to cognition, a knowledge of another's thinking principle." III.

Mr. Manilal says, "Any body's mind can thus be easily comprehended by the *Yogin*.

5. Ability to render the Body Invisible.

Dr. Mitra thus translates Sutra 21 :

"From *Samyama* with reference to the shape of the body, the power of vision being diminished and the correlation of light and sight being severed, there is disappearance." III.

6. Knowledge of the Length of Life and Portents.

Mr. Manilal thus translates and explains Sutra 22:

"*Karma* is of two kinds: active and dormant; by *Samyama* on them (results) knowledge of cessation; as also by portents." III.

"That *karma* which produces its results speedily and is actually on the way to bear fruit is called active; whereas that which is only in a latent condition of potency is called dormant. By performing *Samyama* are these two classes of *karma*, the *Yogin* knows the time of the cessation of his life, *i.e.*, death. He knows at once which *Karma* will produce what fruit, and therefrom at once sees the condition of his death." pp. 65, 66.

It is only Yogins who can properly interpret portents, such as dreams, &c.

7. Ability to enlist the Good-will of any one.

Sutra 23: "In sympathy, &c., strength." III.

By performing *samyama* with reference to sympathy, &c., the goodwill and friendship of any one at any moment may be enlisted.

8. Ability to acquire Strength like that of the Elephant.

Sutra 24: "In strength that of the elephant, &c." III.

By performing *Samyama* on the powers of any animal, the Yogin acquires these powers.

9. Knowledge of hidden Treasures, Mines, &c.

Dr. Mitra thus translates Sutra 25:

"From contemplation of the light of the extremely luminous disposition, a knowledge is acquired of the subtile, the intercepted, and the remote." III.

10. Knowledge of the Sun, Moon, Plants, and Starry Regions.

All this is promised in Sutras 26-28.

11. Knowledge of the Body.

Sutra 29 is as follows:

"In the navel-circle, the knowledge of the arrangement of the body." III.

Hindu physiology makes the navel the grand centre of the body. Great importance is attached to groups of nerves, &c., called *padmas*, supposed to exist in different parts of the body. They are generally supposed to be seven in number, *viz.*, *ádhára* at the anus), *adhisthána* (between the navel and the penis), *manipura*, (at the navel), *anáhata*, (at the heart), *visuddhi*, (in the throat), *ájná* (between the eye-brows), and *sahasrára.*" Mr. Manilal. p. 53.

How far the knowledge of the body acquired by *Yoga* powers is correct, will afterwards be considered.

12. Freedom from Hunger and Thirst.

Sutra 30 says :

"In the pit of the throat the cessation of hunger and thirst." III.

Mr. Manilal gives the following explanation :

"The pit of the throat is the region about the pharynx where the breath from the mouth and nostrils meets. It is said that contact of *prána* with this region produces hunger and thirst, which, therefore may be checked by performing *samyama* on this part to neutralise the effects of the contact." p. 68.

13. Ability to enter another Body.

Sutra 38 says :

"The mind enters another body, by relaxation of the cause of bondage, and by knowledge of the method of passing." III.

It is thus explained by Mr. Manilal :

"The bondage is the *mind's* being bound to a particular body. The cause of limiting the otherwise all-pervading mind to a particular spot is *karma* or *dharma* and *adharma*, *i.e.*, good or bad deeds. When by constant *samyama* on these, the effect of the cause is neutralised and the bonds of confinement loosened, then the mind is free to enter into any dead or living organism and perform its functions through it." p. 71.

14. Ability to rise in the Air.

Sutra 39 says :

"By mastery over *udána*, ascension, and non-contact with water, mud, thorns, &c." III.

Mr. Manilal says :

"The air intercepted between the top of the nose and the heart is called *prána*, that between the heart and the navel is called *samána*, that from the navel to the toes is called *apána*, that above the tip of the nose is called *udána*, and that which pervades the whole body is called *vyána*. The respective functions are—vitalizing, digestion, expulsion of excrements, raising up the sound, &c. and motion in general. The *udána* has a tendency to raise the body upwards, and carry it above water, thorns, &c." p. 72.

15. Ability to Hear at any distance.

Sutra 41 says :

"By *Samyama* on the relation between *ákása*, and the sense of hearing, (arises) supernatural audition." III.

16. Ability to pass through Space.

Sutra 42 says:

"By Samyama on the relation between the body and *ákása*, as also by being identified with light (things like) cotton, (then follows) passage through space." III.

By performing samyama on light things like cotton, the Yogi floats freely in the air.

17. Attainment of the Siddhis.

Sutra 45 says:

"Then the attainment of *animá* and others, as also of perfection of the body and the corresponding non-obstruction of its functions." III.

Siddhis denote high occult powers. Bhoj Raja classifies them under eight heads:

1. *Animá*, ability to reduce one's self to the size of an atom.
2. *Laghima*, ability to become light like cotton.
3. *Garimá*, the power to grow as heavy as desired.
4. *Mahimá*, the power to become any size, so as to be able to touch the moon with the tip of one's finger.
5. *Prákámya*, the irresistible will.
6. *Isatva*, power to create.
7. *Vasitra*, power to command all.
8. *Kamavasayitva*, fulfilment of desires.

18. Mastery over all, Knowledge of all.

Sutra 49 says:

"In him who is fixed upon the distinctive relation of *sattva* and *purusa*, (arise) mastery over all things and the knowledge of all," III.

19. Attainment of Kaivalya.

Sutra 50 says:

"By non-attachment even thereto, follows *Kaivalya*, the seeds of bondage being destroyed." III.

By non-attachment even to occult powers, the Yogi attains *Kaivalya*. This Mr. Manilal defines as "the state of oneness, being one and alone, *viz.*, the *Purusa*." Benfey explains it as "complete absorption in the thought of the universal unity." The causes of bondage destroyed are Ignorance, egoism, desire, aversion, attachment.

BOOK IV.

How the *Siddhis* may be acquired.

Sutra 1 says:

"The Siddhis are produced by birth, herbs, incantations, austerities, or Samádhi." IV.

The *Siddhis*, as already explained, are the occult powers. They may be obtained in various ways:

(*a*) *Birth.* Thus birds at birth have the power of flying.

(*b*) *Herbs.* It is supposed that through certain herbs people may live for ever.

(*c*) *Incantations.* Magical powers are attributed to *mantras*.

(*d*) *Austerities.* The sacred books of the Hindus are full of the wonderful powers exacted from the gods by means of great austerities.

(*e*) *Samádhi.* This is what has been described.

Yogins are not bound by their Actions.

Sutra 7 says:

"Actions are neither white nor black in the case of Yogins; they are of three kinds in the case of others." IV.

Yogins have no attachment; hence they are supposed to be free from the results of their actions. The actions of gods are white, of demons, black; of men, mixed.

How things are known to the Mind.

Sutra 17 says:

"In consequence of the necessity of being tinged by them, things are known or unknown to the mind." IV.

It is a dogma of Hindu Philosophy that the mind is all-pervading. It may therefore be supposed that it can grasp all things at the same time. Such is not the case. It can perceive only those objects into which it is transformed. See p. 6.

Cessation of Desire.

Sutra 25 says:

"The cessation of the desire of knowing the nature of the soul (takes place) in one who has mastered the difference." IV.

In a person who knows the difference between mind and soul and understands the nature and power of either, the desire even of knowing the soul is extinguished. (Mr. Manilal says: "*Kaivalya* is, in fact, a state in which there is entire cessation of all desire." p. 94.)

The "Cloud of Virtue" and the End.

Sutras 29—32 are thus translated by Dr. Mitra:

"On the completion of the series there is produced the meditation called the 'Cloud of Virtue," even in the case of the non-aspirant, from the appearance of constant discrimination. Then follows the cessation of afflictions (or distractions) and works. Then the knowable becomes small from the infiniteness of the knowledge free from all coverings and impurities. Thereupon takes place the termination of the succession of the modifications of the qualities which have accomplished their ends." IV.

Mr. R. C. Bose thus explains the process:

"The devotee first recognizes the fact that his self is different from the thinking principle, and thus attains this discriminative knowledge. Then a shower of virtues or rewards falls upon him unsolicited, in spite of his aspirations being completely withdrawn from them.) Thus the afflictions and works disappear, and the objects of knowledge appear insignificant before its vastness and infinitude. Then the cosmic *gunas* or qualities with all their modifications abandon the soul for ever, or retire leaving the soul in the original state of quiescence and repose. Here is emancipation, the soul's liberation from the trammels of Prakriti till a fresh renovation of the world, if not for ever." p. 183.

The Supreme End to be attained by Yoga.

In some Hindu systems the grand aim is *Sáyujya*, complete union with the Supreme Spirit. Such was not the case with the Sankhya, for it denied, or at least ignored, the existence of Brahma. Patanjali nominally acknowledged his existence, but such union is not the aim of Yoga.

Dr. Mitra says: "The idea of absorption into the godhead, forms no part of the Yoga theory. Patanjali, like Kapila, rests satisfied with the isolation of the soul. He does not pry into the how and the where the soul resides after the separation." (p. 202.)

Patanjali, in his second Sutra, distinctly states that "*Yoga* is the suppression of the transformations of the thinking principle." (Page 4). It is supposed that in consequence of this the union between *purusha* and *prakriti* is dissolved, and there is liberation from future births. To get rid of the curse of existence was the great object of Kapila and Patanjali.

It was at a later period that the doctrine of union arose. There are said to be three inferior conditions leading to it (1) *Sálokya,* living in the same heaven with the personal God: (2) *Sámípya,* close proximity to Him: (3) *Sárúpya,* assimilation to His likeness: (4) *Sáyujya,* complete union. Such an aim is truly noble, and will be hereafter considered.

Before examining the Yoga Sastra of Patanjali, it is desirable to consider the following preliminary subject.

THE CHARACTERISTICS OF THE HINDU MIND.

Nations, like individuals, have their good qualities and their defects. The Indian mind has been at work for about three thousand years, and has created a vast literature in Sanskrit. In some respects it took the lead. Max Müller says: "There were only two nations in the whole history of the world which have conceived independently and without any suggestions from others the two sciences of Logic and Grammar,—the Hindus and the Greeks." In mathematics Indians have the glory of inventing decimal notation, ignorance of which was a great disadvantage to the ancient Greeks and Romans. They likewise possessed an early acquaintance with trigonometry. Sanskrit literature contains numerous passages of great poetical beauty, lofty moral maxims, and sublime descriptions of God. On the other hand, as Sir H. S. Maine, in a Calcutta Convocation Address, when the increased study of Sanskrit was urged upon the Calcutta University, said, "that question is whether we are, or are not, asked under the guise of Oriental Culture, to teach that which is not true—false morality, false history, false philosophy, false physics."

The peculiarities of the Hindu mind which gave rise to these errors will now be noticed.

1. A tendency to Speculate instead of Observe.

Mr. Ram Chandra Bose gives the following examples:

"The Hindu geographer does not travel, does not explore, does not survey; he simply sits down and dreams of a central mountain of a height greater than that of the sun, moon, and stars, and circular oceans of curds and clarified butter. The Hindu historian does not examine documents, coins, and monuments, does not investigate historical facts, weigh evidence, balance probabilities, scatter the chaff to the winds and gather the wheat in his garner: he simply sits down and dreams of a monster monkey who flies through the atmosphere with huge mountains resting on the hairs of his body, and constructs thereby a durable bridge across an arm of an interminable ocean. The Hindu biographer ignores the separating line between history and fable, invents prodigious and fantastic stories, and converts even historical personages into mythical or fabulous heroes. The Hindu anatomist does not dissect, does not anatomize, does not examine the contents of the human body; he simply dreams of component parts which have no existence, multiplies almost indefinitely the number of arteries and veins, and speaks coolly of a passage through which the atomic soul effects its ingress and egress."

"The Hindu metaphysician does not analyze the facts of consciousness or enquire into the laws of thought, does not classify sensations, perceptions, conceptions, and judgments and cautiously proceed to an investigation of the principles which regulate the elaboration of thought and processes of reasoning;—he simply speaks of the mind as an accidental and mischievous adjunct of the soul, and shows how its complete extinction may be brought about by austerity and meditation."*

Hindus claim to have 64 arts and sciences, some of which are the following:

12. The science of prognosticating by omens and augury.
14. The science of healing, which may include restoration to life of the dead, the reunion of severed limbs, &c.
15. Physiognomy, Chiromancy, &c.
36. The art of summoning by enchantment.
37. Exorcism.
38. Exciting hatred between persons by magical spells.
41. The art of bringing one over to another's side by enchantment.
42. Alchemy and chemistry.
44. The language of brute beasts, from ants upwards.
47. Charms against poison.
48. Information regarding any thing lost, obtained by astronomical calculations.
50. The art of becoming invisible.
51. The art of walking in the air.
52. The power of leaving one's own body and entering another lifeless body or substance at pleasure.
56. Restraining the action of fire.
57. The art of walking upon water.
58. The art of restraining the power of wind.
62. The art of preventing the discovery of things concealed.
63. The art by which the power of the sword or any other weapon is nullified.
64. The power of stationing the soul at pleasure in any of the five stages.†

The Brahmanas assert that particular metres have their effects. Thus the Aitareya Brahmana says:

"He who wishes for long life, should use two verses of the *Ushnih* metre (of 28 syllables); for Ushnih is life. He who having such a knowledge uses two Ushnihs arrives at his full age (*i.e.*, 100 years.)

"He who desires strength should use two Trishtubhs' (44 syllables.) Trishtubh is strength, vigour and sharpness of senses. He who knowing this, uses two Trishtubhs, becomes vigour, endowed with sharp senses, and strong.

"He who desires cattle should use two Jagatis (48 syllables). Cattle are Jagati like. He who knowing this uses two Jagatis becomes rich in cattle."‡

A great part of the Atharva Veda consists of supposed magical charms, *e.g.*,

A charm against leprosy.
A charm to obtain invisibility.
A charm to ensure success in gambling.

---

* *Heterodox Philosophy*, pp. 8—10.
† Haug's Translation.

A charm to banish vermin and noxious creatures.
A charm against tigers.
A charm to make a poisoned arrow harmless.
A love charm.
A charm to promote the growth of hair.
A charm to recover a sick man at the point of death.

Belief in the power of charms exists among many nations. A negro baby in West Africa has a charm tied around him soon after he is born, and, as he grows in years, he often adds charm after charm, till his body is covered with them.

In China charms are regularly sold. Charms to secure long life are in great demand. Sometimes the paper on which these charms are written is burnt, and the ashes drunk in water or wine, the result being a very potent charm indeed.

The Japanese carry their charms in bags; the Sinhalese have little cases tied to the body. The Burmese do not require cases for their charms and can never lose them, for there are few who have not charms of some kind tattooed on the arms, back, chest, or even on the top of the head, which is shaved for the purpose. These figures are of all kinds—lizards, birds, mystic words and squares, rings, images of Buddha, and sometimes merely a few scattered dots. The colouring matter is almost always red.

Some of these tattooed charms are supposed to prevent a person from feeling pain when beaten, others guard against danger from snake-bite, musket-shots, drowning, the spells of wizards, and evil spirits. It does not matter to the Burmese although persons having tattooed charms are shot or drowned. Their belief in their efficacy is practically ineradicable.

At an evening meeting in Benares, a Pandit read a paper proving that oil, from its constituents, is heavier than water, in opposition to the lamps burning before his eyes!

Hindus have fallen into all these errors from merely speculating instead of testing their opinions by observation.

2. **Absence of the Historical Faculty.**—The Cambridge Professor of Sanskrit, Mr. E. B. Cowell, says in his Inaugural Lecture:

"We have no such thing as Indian history. Elphinstone has well said, 'No date can be fixed before Alexander's invasion, no connected relation of the national transactions attempted before the Muhammadan conquest.' For history implies a sympathy with the present, and this has never existed in the Hindu mind. The very word history has no corresponding Indian expression. In the Vernaculars derived from the Sanskrit we use the term *itihás;* but how immeasurably different the Sanskrit *itihása* and the Greek *historia!* The one implies personal research and inquiry—its best comment indeed is Herodotus' own life of travel from land to land; the other is a curious compound of three words, *iti, ha, ása,* which almost correspond in meaning to our old nursery phrase, 'there was once upon a time.' In Sanskrit writers the name means simply a legend; it is applied to the mythological traditions of the prose Vedas, or the late heroic poems, as the Mahábhárata; and in defect of any better term, it has been accepted as the native word for history. But its very selection implies that the distinction was unfelt between history and legend. From the earliest ages down to our own day the Hindu mind seems never to have conceived such an idea as an authentic record of past facts based on evidence. It has remained from generation to generation, stationary in that condition which Mr. Grote has described so vividly in the first two volumes of his *History of Greece*. The idlest legend has passed current as readily as the most authentic fact, nay, more readily, because it is more likely to charm the imagination; and in this phase of the mind imagination and feeling supply the only proof which is needed to win the belief of the audience. Hence the whole history of ancient India as a blank."

"Idle legends in later times have arisen, none knows how, to supply some answer to the natural cravings of posterity to know something definite respecting its ancient sages, like those which arose in Greece about Homer and Æsop; but they are the baseless dreams of a lawless popular imagination which sets chronology and geography alike at defiance." pp. 10, 11.

Hindu chronology generally begins with some of the mind-born sons of Brahma. The Vishnu Purana gives an account of the beginning of the solar dynasty; how Daksha was born from the right thumb of Brahma, how Ikswaku was born from the nostril of Manu when he sneezed. The Ramayana describes Dasaratha as reigning 60,000 years.

3. **A want of Common Sense.**—This indeed is almost characteristic of "philosophers." Cicero long ago remarked, "There is nothing so absurd, but it may be said by a philosopher."

Hindu philosophers framed certain theories, and then proceeded to draw from them a long train of conclusions. Whether they were consistent with common sense, it did not seem to enter into their minds to inquire. Indeed, as Sir Monier Williams says, "the more evidently physical and metaphysical speculations are opposed to common sense, the more favour do they find with some Hindu thinkers. Common sense tells an Englishman that he really exists himself and that everything he sees around him really exists also. He cannot abandon these two primary convictions. Not so the Hindu Vedantist."

The sacred writings of the Hindus abound with contradictions, but this gives no trouble. Max Müller says: "The same god is sometimes represented as supreme, sometimes as equal, sometimes as inferior to others. The father is sometimes the son, the brother is the husband, and she who in one hymn is the mother as in another the wife." The most extraordinary feat is ascribed to Indra, "Thou hast indeed begotten thy father and mother together from thy own body." As Max Müller remarks: "A god who once could do that was no doubt capable of anything afterwards."

One result of this want of common sense, is *boundless credulity*.

In the Ramayana Hanuman tears up a Himalayan mountain by the roots, and transports it through the air to Lanka. Before returning to Rama from Lanka, he ascended Mount Arishta. Pressed by his enormous weight, it uttered cries of distress, and sank down from the height of 30 yojanas, (about 210 miles) to the level of the earth!

4. **Accepting Illustration for Argument.**—Max Müller, describes the late Ramakrishna as a "real Mahatman," and gives extracts from his precepts. The following is an example:

> (11) As one can ascend the top of a house by means of a ladder, or a bamboo, or a staircase, or a rope, so divers are the ways, and means to approach God, and every religion in the world shows one of these ways."*

This is a mere variation of the well-known saying: "As there are several roads to the same city, so all religions lead to God."

Ramkrishna's argument amounts to this, As there are several ways of getting to the top of a house, so the most contradictory statements are all true. The logic of this is mere drivelling.

The main proof adduced for the doctrine of Maya is that a rope may be mistaken for a snake, or that in a dream things appear to be real.

5. **A proneness to dwell on subtle distinctions instead of grasping a subject as a whole.**—The Hindu mind resembles that of Hudibras,

> "He could distinguish and divide
> A hair 'twixt south and south-west side."

One great difference between a good and a bad lawyer is that the latter takes up some subordinate point, while he fails to see the main issue on which the case turns. Sir Monier Williams says that a Hindu disputant has captious propensities, leading him to be quick in repartee, and ready with specious objections to the most conclusive arguments. Mr. R. C. Bose says, even of the Hindu master-minds, that they were defective in the following respects:—

> "A view broad and comprehensive, an investigation calm and persevering, a thorough sifting of evidence, and a cautious building up of generalisations, in a word for all those processes of research and reasoning which are the basis of reliable science."†

6. **Acceptance of false Premises.**—One Hindu dogma is the denial of *creation* in the proper sense of the word. Because man cannot create (call objects into existence) therefore God cannot. Hence the eternal Prakriti. Another dogma is the eternal existence of the soul. Hence the weary round of transmigration.

---

* *The Nineteenth Century*, August, 1896.
† *Heterodox Philosophy*, p. 7.

Mr. Bose says of Hindu philosophers :

"They had an intellect keen and argumentative, and their writings are fitted to raise the puzzling question, so well put by Lord Macaulay, viz., how men, who reason so closely and so consecutively from assumed premises fail so miserably to see the utter groundlessness of the assumptions on which their ably conducted arguments are based."

7. **Proud attempts to solve questions beyond the range of the human intellect**; *e. g.* the nature of the soul, hereafter noticed.

Dr. Murray Mitchell notices :

"The hard dogmatism and the unbounded self-assertion of all the schools. It would be an immense relief if one word betokening distrust of their own wisdom were uttered by those teachers—such as we have heard occasionally proceeding from the Vedic poets ; but there is no such word. Each theorist moves with head erect, possessed of absolute faith in his own omniscience. It never occurs to him either that there are matters with which the human mind had no faculties to deal, or that Truth unveils her treasures only to the humble."*

Their vagaries are even asserted to have a divine origin.

"The Hindu philosopher," says Mr. Bose, "claims prophetic functions, pretends to either miraculous insight or preternatural intercourse with superior beings, and brings out his excogitation as revelation to be implicitily believed in ; not as results of philosophic inquiry to be tested by the ordinary appliances of the logical science. He is the guru, heaven-appointed or self-raised teacher, and his utterances must be accepted as divine revelations ; while all sorts of woes are pronounced

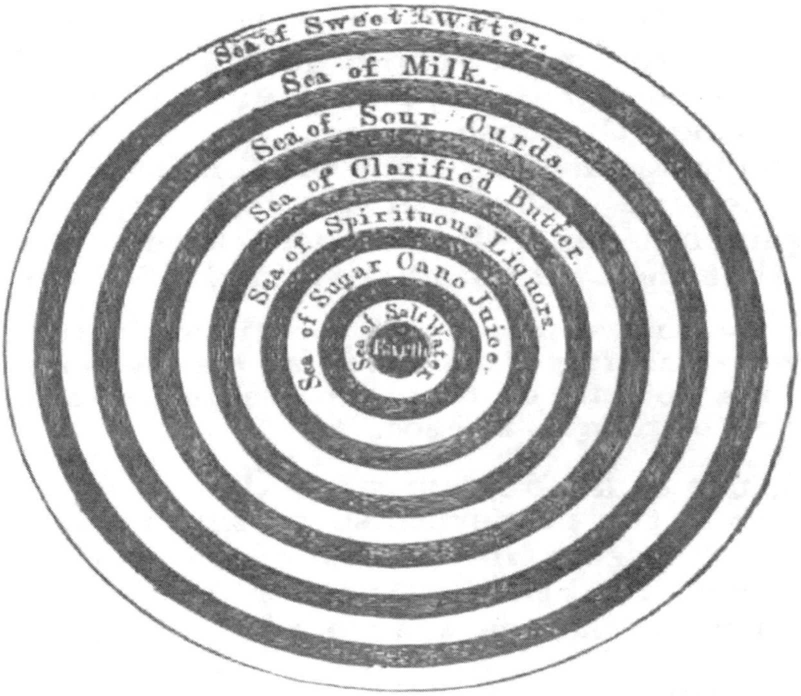

* Hinduism, p. 83.

upon those impious wretches who have the audacity to call in question a jot or tittle of his sayings."

Some of the false teaching of Hinduism will now be considered.

FALSE GEOGRAPHY OF THE SASTRAS.

The following description of the earth is given in the Vishnu Purana, Book II. Chap. 2:

"The 7 great insular continents are Jambu, Plaksha, Salmali, Kusa, Krauncha, Saka, and Pushkara. They are surrounded severally by 7 great seas, the sea of salt water (Lavana), of sugarcane juice (Ikshu), of wine (Sura), of clarified butter (Sarpi), of curd (Dadhi), of milk, (Dugdha), and of fresh water (Jala)."

"Jambudwipa is in the centre of all these: and in the centre of this continent is the golden mountain Meru. The height of Meru is 84,000 yojanas; and its depth below the surface of the earth is 16,000. Its diameter at the summit is 32,000 yojanas; and at its base, 16,000; so that this mountain is like the seed-cup of the lotus of the earth."

FALSE ASTRONOMY OF THE SASTRAS.

According to the Vishnu Purana (Book II. Chap. 7.) the distances of the planets are as follows:

The sphere of the earth extends as far as it is illuminated by the rays of the sun and moon; and to the same extent is the sphere of the atmosphere (Bhuvar loka) spread above it. The solar orb is situated 100,000 yojanas from the earth; and that of the moon an equal distance from the sun. At the same interval above the moon occurs the orbit of all the lunar constellations. The planet Budha (Mercury) is 200,000 yojanas above the lunar mansions. Sukra (Venus) is at the same distance from Mercury. Angaraka (Mars) is as far above Venus; and the priest of the gods (Vrihaspati, or Jupiter) as far from Mars; while Saturn (Sani) is 250,000 yojanas beyond Jupiter The sphere of the 7 Rishis (Ursa Major) is 100,000 yojanas above Saturn; and at a similar height above the Rishis is Dhruva (the pole star), the pivot or axis of the whole planetary circle.

It will be seen that the sun is represented as a lakh of yojanas from the earth, and the moon as a lakh of yojanas beyond the sun. On the contrary, the moon is only about 240,000 miles from the earth; whereas the distance of the sun is about 91 millions of miles. The other distances given are equally erroneous.

FALSE ACCOUNTS OF THE BODY.

The ancient Hindus thought that a man was rendered impure by touching a dead body. Hence they did not dissect and examine it minutely as is done in modern Medical Colleges. The writers of the Upanishads simply framed an imaginary body out of their own heads, and, to impose upon the ignorant, said that it had been revealed by Brahma.

Dr. Webb says: The anatomical knowledge of the Hindus may be judged of by a single sentence:—*viz.*, the navel is the origin of all the vessels, and is the principal seat of life."*

The Katha Upanishad contains the following :—

"16. There are hundred and one arteries of the heart; the one of them (Susumná,) proceeds to the head. By this (at the time of death) rising upwards (by the door of A'ditya) a person gains immortality; or the other (arteries) are of various course."

A similar statement is made in the Chhandogya Upanishad:

"There are a hundred and one arteries issuing from the heart; one of them penetrates the crown of the head. The man who departs this life through that artery, secures immortality. The rest of the arteries lead to *various* transitions,—they lead to *various* transitions." VIII. 6.6.

The Prasna Upanishad gives the following additional details:

"For the (ether of the) heart is verily that soul. There (arise) the hundred and one (principal) arteries; each of them is hundred times divided; 72,000 are the branches of every branch artery; within them moves the circulating air." III. 6.

The whole number of arteries is therefore 727,200,000!

The slightest examination of the heart shows that all this is purely imaginary. There are just two branches of a large artery from the heart, containing impure blood, leading to the lungs, and one great artery, which, afterwards, subdivided, conveys pure blood, to the whole body. In like manner, there are two great veins carrying impure blood to the heart from the whole body, and four veins, containing pure blood, leading from the lungs to the heart.

The Prasna Upanishad says that "within the arteries moves the circulating air." *Arteries* mean air-pipes. They were thought to contain only air, because after death they are empty. When a person is alive, blood flows through them. This is proved by the fact that if one of them is cut, blood gushes out. When a person dies, the heart loses its power to send out blood, and the arteries are found empty.

Inference from the Foregoing Statements.

No educated Hindu can deny that the statements in the shastras about the earth, the solar system, and the human body are false, confirming the assertion of Sir H. S. Maine previously quoted. When a witness is convicted of false testimony on some points,

---

* *Hindu System of Medicine* by Wise. p. 214.

discredit is thrown upon the rest of his statements. There is a presumption that the Yoga Sutras of Patanjali, may be as unreliable as the Vishnu Purana. This will now be established.

EXAMINATION OF THE YOGA SUTRAS.

1. Object of Patanjali.

As already explained, according to Patanjali, "All is misery." (page 10). The grand object therefore is to cut short the transmigrations. Patanjali promises to do this by "*Yoga*—the suppression of the transformations of the thinking principle."

Hindu philosophy contains many speculations about the soul, some of which may be quoted.

The soul is generally supposed to be of the size of the thumb, and to dwell in the heart, but it is considered also both infinitely small and infinitely great, as will be shown by the following quotations:

12. The soul (Purusha) which in the measure of a thumb dwells in the middle of the body (in the ether of the heart) is the ruler of the past, the future (and the present time.) Hence from having this knowledge, the wise (does not desire to conceal) the soul (*vide* latter part of v. 5). This is that.*

13. He is the perfect spirit (Purusha), of the measure of a thumb, the inner soul, who always abides in the heart of every man, the ruler of knowledge, who is concealed by the heart and mind. Those who know him; become immortal.†

8. He, who, of the measure of a thumb, resembling the sun in splendour, endowed with determination and self-consciousness, and with the quality of intellect and the quality of his body, is perceived even as another (different from the universal soul, although it is one with it) only like the iron thong at the end (of a whip.)

9. The embodied soul is to be thought like the hundredth part of the point of a hair, divided into hundred parts; he is considered to be infinite.‡

3. Is the soul within me; it is lighter than a corn, or a barley, or a mustard, or a canary seed, or the substance within it. Such a soul is within me, as is greater than this earth, and greater than the sky, and greater than the heaven, and greater than all these regions [put together.] §

The Vaiseshika school maintains that the soul is diffused everywhere through space. "Akasa, in consequence of its universal pervasion, is infinitely great; and so likewise is soul." VII. 22.

---

* *Katha Upanishad.* IV. 2. 12.
† *Swetaswatara Upanishad.* III. 13.
‡ *Swetaswatara Upanishad.* V. 8, 9.
§ *Chhandogya Upanishad.* III. 14, 3.

Nehemiah Goreh well remarks: "Those who believe that the soul of a musquito fills heaven and earth, can believe anything." Sir A. C. Lyall justly describes "boundless credulity" as one of the characteristics of Hinduism. The transformations of the thinking principle is another dogma of Hindu philosophy. The thinking principle, the mind, is supposed to be transformed or changed into the object it sees. Photographs are taken by means of an instrument, somewhat like the human eye. A little picture of the objects around us is formed on the inner part of the eye. In some wonderful way this picture is conveyed by a nerve to the brain and we see it. Other nerves convey impressions of hearing, smell, taste, and touch. It is absurd to suppose that the mind is transformed into what we perceive by the senses.

But "the suppression of the transformations of the thinking principle" may simply be understood to mean that the mind is to cease to act. To secure this the directions are given, first to concentrate the mind on one object, and at last to meditate without an object or on nothing. This virtually means that we are to try to reduce ourselves to the state we are when fast asleep, conscious of nothing. If Hindu pessimism is correct, that "all is misery," this state is desirable; but if, on the contrary, existence may be "happiness," it is the reverse.

MEANS OF ATTAINMENT.

1. Yama (*Restraint.*)

The explanatory Sutra is as follows:

"Yama includes abstinence from slaughter, falsehood, theft, incontinence, and avarice." II. 30.

Mr. Manilal rightly helds that unholy thoughts are condemned as well as unholy deeds. Abstinence from all sin is our duty, and we should use every effort in our power to avoid it. The error of Patanjali is to ignore divine help,—to make man his own saviour. Every one who has honestly tried to overcome sin knows the immense difficulty of the task. A Hindu writer says: "This powerful devil of a deceitful heart is fiercer than fire, more impassable than the mountains, and harder than adamant: sooner might the ocean be emptied than the mind restrained."

2. Niyama (*Obligation.*)

Niyama is thus explained:

"The obligations are purity, contentment, penance, study, and devotion to Isvara." II. 32.

"Cease to do evil" is not sufficient: "learn to do well," ought to follow. We should not simply try to avoid evil actions, but seek the opposite virtues. The great question is, how can these virtues be attained? The means recommended by Patanjali will next be considered.

3. Asana (*Posture.*)

Asana and its results are thus explained:

"Posture is that which is firm and pleasant. By mild effort and meditation on the endless. Then no assults from the pairs of opposites." II. 46-48.

The pairs of opposites are heat and cold, pleasure and pain, &c., which are no longer felt.

Our bodies, as the Bible says: are "fearfully and wonderfully made." One of the most remarkable of the organs is the brain and other parts of what are called the "nervous system." The brain has been compared to the telegraph office of the body, from which the nerves go to all parts to convey orders. The nerves are very small cords, somewhat like threads, composed of the same substance as the brain.

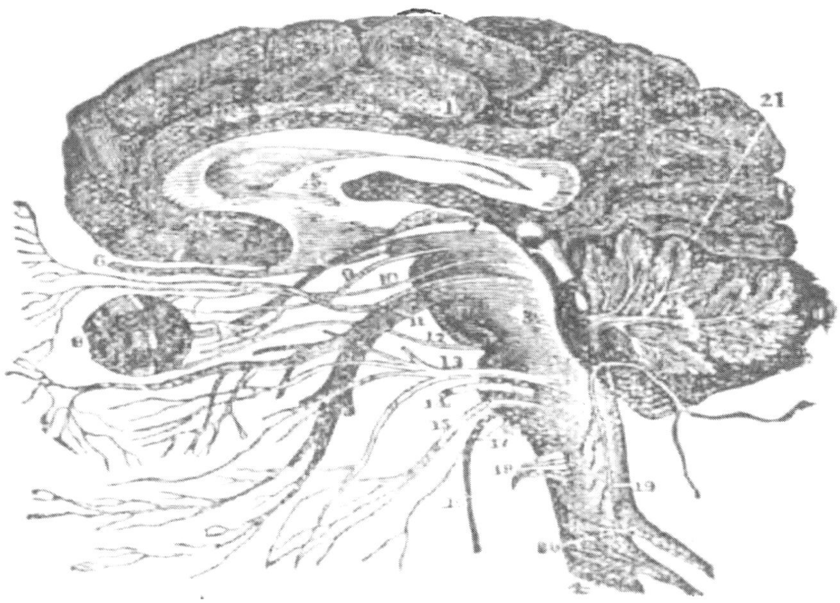

SECTION OF THE BRAIN.

There are two principal kinds—nerves of *motion* and nerves of *sensation*. The muscles, the fleshy parts, move the limbs; but they receive their orders from the nerves, and cannot act without them. In the disease, called palsy, or paralysis, the power of motion is lost, though pain is felt,—the nerves of motion alone being affected. In other cases the nerves of sensation are affected, and then boiling water gives no pain. The nerves of sensation are of different kinds; as touch, sight, hearing, smell, taste. We commonly say that the eye sees; but the eye may be perfect, if the nerves leading from it to the brain is injured, we cannot see. In the engraving the eye is marked 8; from the ball a nerve is seen going to the brain. Strictly speaking, it is the brain which sees, hears, &c. It is the organ of the mind.

The cause of *sleep* is still a mystery. Chambers's *Encyclopædia* says: "For upwards of two thousand years continuous attempts have been made to elucidate the cause of sleep without success; many theories have been promulgated, but they have fallen short of explaining it."

There are several stages of sleep and varieties in the action of the brain, some of which may be noticed.

Brown Study.—This is a state of meditation directed to no certain object. It may be called a waking dream.

Dreaming.—This state is caused by the partial activity of the brain. Ideas are not corrected by the external senses; common sense seems completely lost; the most wonderful things excite no surprise.

Mesmeric or Hypnotic Sleep.—This is a kind of artificial sleep, in which there is an unusual suspension of some of the powers and an unusual activity of others. It has various stages. The person may be more or less under its influence.

The sense of feeling is lost, and a limb may be taken off unknown to the person. Dr. Esdale, of Calcutta, had charge of a hospital in which operations were performed in this way for years. It is not now employed, as the same effect can be more readily produced by chloroform.

Catalepsy.—This is a sudden suspension of the senses, and the body becomes fixed like a statue. The nerves of motion seem to be curiously affected.

Delirium.—This is a violent excitement of the mental faculties. It may be caused by the brain being inflamed by strong drink, by fever, &c.

Dreamless Natural Sleep.—In this state all the mental faculties are at rest.

Coma.—This is a total loss of power of thought or motion, from which the patient cannot be aroused. It is generally caused by the bursting of a blood vessel in the brain.

Yoga Sastra aims to promote hypnotic sleep. Eighty-four postures are enumerated. These have no influence: the real effect is produced by looking steadily at the tip of the nose or between the eyebrows. In Europe persons to be hypnotised are told simply to look fixedly at one point.

A well known expedient to induce sleep is to repeat again and again the same word. A noted English bishop used for this purpose the vowels, *a*, *e*, *i*, *o*. These he repeated till he dropped off to sleep. Dr. Radcliff says that a boy put himself to sleep by pronouncing the word *cup* 450 times.

Yoga Sastra employs the same means. Sutra 28 Book I. enjoins the constant repetition of *Om*. (See page 7). Sutra 44 Book II. says "By study (is produced) communion with the desired deity." Mr. Manilal explains "study as the constant, silent, and devoted repetition of certain formulæ." p. 49.

Dr. Paul, in his *Yoga Philosophy,* gives the following directions for the *Siddhásana :*

"Place the left heel under the anus and the right heel in front of the genitals; fix the sight upon the space between the eyebrows, and while in this motionless attitude, meditate upon the syllable Om, a mysterious word, the frequent inaudible repetition of which is said to ensure release from worldly existence." pp. 26, 27.

Dr. Paul adds:

"The *Siddhásana* and *Padmásana* are both tranquil and quiet postures, favouring a tranquil circulation and slow respiration. In those postures the Yogis sit and pronounce inaudibly the hypnotic syllable Om, and meditate upon it in order to tranquillize circulation and retard the respiratory movements." p. 27.

Other syllables may also be repeated. Dr. Paul says:

"A Yogi is directed to pronounce inaudibly the mantras, Bam, Sam, and Lam, 600 times. He then pronounces Bam, Bham, Yam, Ram, and Lam, 6000 times. He next pronounces Dam, Dham, Nam, Tam, Tham, Dam, Dham, Nam, Pam, and Pham, 6000 times. He then pronounces inaudibly Kam, Kham, Gam, Gham, Nam, Cham, Chham, Jam, Jham, Nam, Tam, and Tham. He then pronounces inaudibly Am, Am, I'm, I'm, Um, Um, Rim, Dïm, Lrim, Lrim, Em, Aim, Om, Aum, Am, 6000 times. And lastly he utters inaudibly Hansa, 2000 times." p. 28.

Fixing the eye on the tip of the nose and the repetition of the same syllable tend to produce hypnotic sleep, in which, it is true, "the transformations of the thinking principle are suppressed" for a time as in natural sleep. The brain ceases to act. As in natural sleep, neither hunger nor thirst, &c. is felt. Whether this is a desirable condition to which a human being should reduce himself, will afterwards be considered.

PRANAYAMA.

The Yoga Sastra attaches very great importance to *pránáyáma,* the regulation of the breath.

It has been shown that the Sastras give most incorrect accounts of the arteries, based on speculation. Assertions about the breath display the same ignorance.

Some introductory remarks may be made.

Why we breathe.—The blood in its course through the body both nourishes us and carries away waste matter. It leaves the lungs a bright red colour; when it returns to the lungs, after passing through the body, it is dark-coloured from the waste matter it has picked up. How is it purified? The air is composed mainly of two gases, called *Oxygen* and *Nitrogen.* The oxygen is that which supports life. When we breathe, the oxygen goes down into the lungs; it unites with the waste matter of the blood, and carries it away, leaving it pure. The product formed by the oxygen and the waste-matter is called carbonic acid gas. It forms about 4 parts in a hundred of the air given out. Suppose a person were shut up in a close room, 6 feet square, into which no fresh air could enter; the oxygen in the air would gradually be consumed, being replaced by carbonic acid gas, and the person would die. The same result follows more rapidly when people are hanged or drowned. The blood is not purified by the air; only the dark blood goes round and round, so they soon lose their senses and die.

The stage of insensibility before death may be reached by breathing the same air over and over again. This is known to the Yogas as *Pránapana Yoga.* It is one of the easiest means of reaching Samádhi.

Object of Pranayama.—As already explained, drawing in the breath is called *Puraka;* giving it out is called *Rechaka;* the interval between is called *Kumbhaka.* According to Yoga Sastra, whatever prolongs Kumbhaka promotes longevity. Hence one great object of Pránáyáma is to lengthen this interval.

Animals which breathe rapidly consume much oxygen, give out much carbonic acid, and are warmer than those which breathe more slowly. A pigeon breathes about 34 times a minute, a man 16 times, a tortoise 3 times. A pigeon is warmer blooded than a human being, and dies of hunger in three days; a tortoise feels cold to the touch and can live for months without food. Through *Pránáyáma* a man breathes much less frequently even than a tortoise.

Dr. Paul gives the length of the inspiration, interval and expiration in each of the following stages:

Duration in Seconds.

		Inspiration.	*Intervals.*	*Expiration.*
Pránáyáma	...	12 seconds.	324 seconds.	24 seconds.
Pratyáhára	...	do.	648 do.	do.
Dhyárana	...	do.	1296 do.	do.
Dhyána	...	do.	2592 do.	do.
Samádhi	...	do.	5184 do.	do.

Yogis living for weeks without food.—Cases have been known in which Yogis have been shut up for 40 days without food. This was done in the time of Ranjit Singh. The following is the explanation :

There is an animal found in the Himalayas, somewhat like a rabbit, called the marmot. For five months in the year the region where it lives is covered with snow, and food cannot be obtained. It then retreats to a small den, filled with straw and dry leaves of plants to keep it warm, and with the opening carefully covered up. The marmot has a long narrow tongue, the point of which is turned back to the gullet, closing almost entirely the passage to the lungs. In this state the animal sleeps till the return of spring. It is called *hibernating* or wintering, and is practised by several animals in cold countries. In that state the animals slowly consume the fat of their bodies. The bear when it begins to hibernate is fat ; when it awakes, it is lean.

Some Yogis have learned to imitate the Himalayan marmot. The preparatory process is called *Khechari mudra*. It consists in cutting a part of the tongue, called the bridle, and drawing it out till it is lengthened and can be turned back to the gullet. As the marmot has its den, so the Yogi has his *guphá*, or underground retreat, carefully stopped up to exclude the air. Like the marmot, the Yogí prepares his bed from Kusa grass, cotton and the wool of sheep, and, like it, he turns back his tongue. In this way he can exist for some time in a low state of vitality, the consumption of oxygen being reduced to a minimum.*

SUPPOSED OCCULT POWERS.

Yoga is chiefly valued by the Hindus as it is supposed that, through means of it, magical powers can be acquired, a list of the principal of which has been given. See pp. 25-27. This belief, like that in mantras and incantations, arises from the want of observation. If the supposed powers had been tested, their baselessness would have been discovered.

The actual results of *Pránáyáma* are as follows : The blood is imperfectly purified, and the person may fall into a dreamy state in which he may suppose that he wanders about and does wonderful things. Savages believe that the soul actually leaves the body in dreams. They dislike awaking a person lest his soul should miss its way back to its body. By continuing the process, the vitality may be reduced to that of the hibernating marmot. The "transformations of the thinking principle are suppressed," because the Yogi has been brought to a state of insensibility bordering on death.

Professor Wilson, a noted Oriental Scholar, says of Yogis and Yoga Sastra :

"They specially practise the various gesticulations and postures of

* Abridged from Dr. Paul's *Yoga Philosophy*.

which it consists, and labour assiduously to suppress their breath and fix their thoughts until the effect does somewhat realize expectation, and the brain, in a state of overwrought excitement, bodies forth a host of crude and wild conceptions, and gives to airy nothingness a local habitation and a name." *Hindu Sects.* p. 132.

Barth, a distinguished French Orientalist, says of Yoga exercises:

"Conscientiously observed they can only issue in folly and idiocy." *Religions of India.* p. 83.

About sixty years a Madras Brahman professed, by yoga powers, to be able to sit in the air without support. First a tent was erected, and when removed he was seen, as in the frontispiece, counting his beads, with his hand resting upon a Yoga-*danda* or staff. The explanation is simple. The staff was a hollow bamboo, with an iron rod inside, which at the top was so bent as to form a seat for the Yogi. The iron rod was fixed firmly in the ground while covered by the tent, which was only removed when the preparations had been completed. Such feats of jugglery may be seen any day in London.

Colonel Olcott had heard in America of the wonderful doings of Yogis, and on his arrival in India wished to see proofs of their magic powers. He describes those he saw as "painted impostors, who masquerade as *Sadhus*, to cheat the charitable, and secretly give loose to their beastly nature."*

Reward of Rs. 1,000.

A reward of the above sum is offered to any Yogi who will, by yoga power, raise himself in the air 3 feet and remain suspended for ten minutes. The conditions are that it must be done in the open air and by daylight. There must be no rod connecting him with the ground nor any balloon above his head.

J. Murdoch.

Madras, *October* 1896.

The Hindu belief in the power of Yoga, mantras, and charms is all a delusion.

Hindu Pessimism and False View of Life.

It has been shown that the first Sutra of the Sánkhya system is that "the complete cessation of pain is the complete end of man." As existence is a curse, this is to be secured by freedom from future births. The Yoga Sastra, and indeed every system of Hindu philosophy, takes a similar gloomy view of life. "To the enlightened all is misery," says Patanjali (II. 15).

* *Lectures*, p. 184.

The general belief is that this is the Kali Yuga, succeeding supposed Krita, Treta, and Dwapara Yugas, representing golden, silver, brazen, and iron ages. The doleful account of the Kali Yuga given in the Vishnu Purana has been quoted. Among other things, "a man will be grey when he is 12, and no one will exceed 20 years of life." All this only shows the absence of the historical faculty among the Hindus. Like little children, they have accepted the most improbable legends as true.

There never was a golden age in India. The earliest inhabitants were savages, ignorant of the metals, who fought with each other and wild beasts with arrows tipped with flint. This is shown by the flint arrow heads which have been dug up all over India, and may be seen in museums. Only very gradually did civilization arise and spread. Even under the most celebrated Hindu sovereigns, as Macaulay says, "We see the multitudes sunk in brutal ignorance and the studious few engaged in acquiring what did not deserve the name of knowledge." The Brahmans sought to confine all learning to themselves. The country was without roads or bridges; there was not a single printed book or a newspaper. India was never richer, more civilized or more prosperous than at present. Instead of things becoming worse and worse, every year improvements are made. Human ignorance and sin are the great sources of human sorrow. Remove these, and existence, instead of being a curse, will be a blessing. The burning words of Kingsley ought to be impressed upon the minds of all:

"Foremost among them stands a law which I must insist on, boldly and perpetually, a law which man has been trying in all ages, as now, to deny, or at least to ignore; though he might have seen it if he had willed, working steadily in all times and nations. And that is—that as the fruit of righteousness is wealth and peace, strength and honour; the fruit of unrighteousness is poverty and anarchy, weakness and shame. It is an ancient doctrine and yet one ever young."*

In England, during the last two centuries, the average duration of life has doubled, while the general standard of comfort has been remarkably raised. Our happiness depends very much upon ourselves. "Godliness is profitable unto all things, having promise of the life that now is, and of that which is to come." We may be happy in this world, and unspeakably happy for ever in the next.

Brief Examination of the Sankhya System.

Before taking up Yoga Sastra, a few remarks may be offered on Kapila's philosophy.

1. **Its low selfish end.**—This is simply "the complete cessation of pain." A far higher aim is to try to become wiser and

---

* *Limits of Exact Science applied to History.*

better, more useful to all around us, or to seek communion with God.

2. **Its absurd ascription of distinguishing qualities to some material objects.**—Sound is said to be the characteristic of *ákása,* ether. Light makes its way from the sun through *ákása,* but we have no reason to believe that it conveys sound. Tremendous explosions take place on the surface of the sun; but the faintest murmur of them never reaches the earth. The eternity of sound is another figment of Hindu philosophy. Extension would have been a fitter characteristic for *ákása.* "Earth is that which has the quality of *odour.*" Dry earth has no smell. One would have supposed that *solidity* would rather have been mentioned. *Taste* is said to be the distinguishing quality of water! Pure water is tasteless; any taste is caused by the presence of salt or some other substance. Fluidity is rather its characteristic in its ordinary state.

3. **Its infinite number of eternal existences.**—Hindu philosophy assigns two causes for the eternity of the soul:

One argument is the supposed axiom: "Whatever exists must always have existed." This denies God's omnipotence. "Thou thoughtest that I was altogether such an one as thyself." A carpenter cannot work without materials; in like manner it is supposed that God must have formed all things out of eternally existing matter. "Ye do err, not knowing the power of God. By His will He can create things or call them out of nothing into existence.

Another argument is that "Whatever had a beginning must have an end." This is also a denial of God's power. He can give a future eternal existence to any creature He has called into being. According to Hinduism, souls may pass into gods, demons, beasts, birds, reptiles, fishes, insects, into plants, and even into inanimate objects. "Who can estimate the number of these eternal *svayambhu* essences! Is it not perfectly unphilosophical, because absolutely unnecessary and egregiously extravagant, to assume such an indefinite number of eternal essences, when one Supreme Essence is sufficient to account for all things, visible or invisible, material or spiritual?"*

4. **Its Atheism.**—It is true that Sutra 93 "*Iswaráseddhih.* The existence of Iswara is a thing unproved," seems only agnostic; but the possiblity of His existence is denied in the next Sutra: "If free and unbound, He cannot be either, and therefore cannot exist."†

Prakriti, itself unintelligent, is supposed to be the author of their universe, so wonderfully formed that after thousands of years, the most learned men are still ignorant, in many respects, of its structure. To every intelligent, thoughtful man, the atheism of any

* Banerjea's *Dialogues,* p. 164.

† Quoted by Dr. Mullens, *Hindu-Philosophy.* pp. 181, 182.

system is a sufficient ground for its rejection. Proofs of the existence of God will be found clearly stated in *The Existence and Character of God* by Row.*

THE TRUE YOGA SASTRA.

Patanjali's system has been examined. The one which should take its place will now be explained.

ITS AIM.

Instead of seeking "the suppression of the transformations of the thinking principle," by want of exercise, fixing eye on the tip of the nose, and breathing like a tortoise, we should try to render our bodily and mental powers as perfect as possible. The maxim of the greatest nation of antiquity was, "A sound mind in a sound body." They are to be used, however, not in acquiring wealth or power, but in doing the greatest amount of good we can to all around us.

YAMA.

The restraint of all our evil passions is our bounden duty. One great help to this is temperance. The body should not be pampered by luxurious living; abstinence from all intoxicating liquors is a great safeguard. Companions or places that would lead us astray ought to be shunned. Above all, we should seek divine help. "Watch and pray that ye enter not into temptation;" "Hold Thou me up, and I shall be safe.

NIYAMA.

Virtues should be cultivated as well as vices restrained. The Bible says; "Whatsoever things are true, whatsoever things are honest, whatsoever things are just, whatsoever things are pure, whatsoever things are lovely, whatsoever things are of good report; if there be any virtue, and if there be any praise, think on these things." Elsewhere it is said, "add to your faith virtue." *Virtue* comes from *vir*, 'a man.' Its primary meaning is manliness; among the Romans *virtus* meant bravery. In India it may be understood as moral courage, faithfulness to one's convictions of duty. No virtue is more needed among educated Hindus.

ASANA.

Suppose a master intrusts to a servant an instrument wonderfully constructed to enable him to do his work; he will expect him to take care of it and keep it in proper order. If, instead of

* Sold by Mr. A. T. Scott, ½ Anna.

that, he tried to weaken its powers and render it useless, he would be considered very blameworthy. The body is that instrument committed to us by God to do His will. Instead of being enfeebled, it should be made as strong and healthy as possible.

Ignorant Hindus believe that it is a work of merit to hold up the arm till the muscles becomes withered from want of exercise, and the arm is rendered powerless. Compare, on the other hand, the arm of a blacksmith who wields a heavy hammer, how well the muscles are developed! By Yoga postures, the muscles are cramped and deprived of exercise: while the Yogi is looking at the tip of his nose, and muttering syllables which promote hypnotic sleep.

The true *ásana* are gymnastic exercises to develop the different muscles. When recruits enter the army, they are practised on them, with the result of considerably increasing their strength. They have been wisely introduced into some schools. Cricket and other games answer the same purpose. Elderly persons may take a walk. Hindus would be much healthier, live longer, and suffer less from diabetes, if they took sufficient exercise.

Pranayama.

Mr. Manilal's remarks have been quoted:

"*Udgháta* appears to mean the rising of the breath from the navel, and its striking at the roof of the palate. *Pránáyáma* has as its chief object the mixing of *prána*, the upper breath, and *apána*, the lower breath, and raising them upwards by degrees and stages till they subside on the head. This practice awakens a peculiar force which is dormant about the navel, and is called *Kundalini*. It is this force which is the source of all occult power." p. 52.

Sankarácharyá in his *Atmánátma Vivekah*, as translated by Mr. Mohinee M. Chatterjee, thus describes the "five vital airs:"

"*Prána, apána, vyána, udána and samána*. Their locations are said to be:—of *prána*, the breast, of *apána* the fundament, of *samána* the navel, of *udána*, the throat, and *vyána* is spread all over the body. Functions of these are:—*prána* goes out, *apána* descends, *udána* ascends, *samána* reduces the food eaten into an undistinguishable state, and *vyána* circulates all over the body. Of these five vital airs there are five sub-airs, namely *nága, kúrma, krikara, devadatta and dhananjaya*. Functions of these are: eructations produced by *nága*, *kúrma* opens the eye, *dhananjaya* assimilates food, *devadatta* causes yawning, and *krikara* produces appetite—this is said by those versed in *Yoga*."*

All this is only shows crass ignorance of the structure of the body. No breath goes down to the navel, so it cannot be raised. The *prána* and *apána* are sheer nonsense; as is the "dormant force about the navel." Belief in "occult powers" will afterwards be

* *Compendium of the Raja Yoga Philosophy*, published by Tookaram Tatya, Bombay, pp. 40, 41.

noticed. Some account will now be given of breathing and its uses.

The muscles and brain require to be nourished as well as exercised. Pure blood is the chief means. Instead of the *small supply of impure air* afforded by the yoga exercises, we should aim at a *large supply of pure air.* How is this to be secured? The air we breathe goes down into the lungs, which are full of small air cells, somewhat like a sponge. As a sponge is much larger when its cells are filled with water than when dry, so the lungs swell out when their cells are filled with air. How many little air cells are there in the lungs? About sixty lakhs! The air after staying a little time in the air cells, goes out again. We can see our breasts rise and fall as the air enters and leaves.

It has been explained that it is the oxygen in the air which purifies the blood and removes waste matter. The yoga exercises seek to diminish its supply. The object should be the very reverse. When people lean forward the air cells in the lungs are compressed and admit a smaller quantity of air. To increase their capacity, the shoulders should be thrown back; we should then slowly inhale as much air as we can to distend the lungs; hold it for some time and then exhale it. Such an exercise practised a dozen times a day, would permanently increase the capacity of the chest, and render a person stronger and healthier. When soldiers enter the army, their girth at the chest is measured. After a time, by means of such exercises, it has been found to increase about two inches or more.

Herbert Spencer says, "The first requisite to success in life is to be a good animal"—that is to have a strong healthy body. If India is to rise in the scale of nations, instead of admiring dreaming ascetics, weak both in body and mind, she must try to produce men like Prince Ranjit Singh, able to complete successfully with Englishmen at their national game of cricket.

Disbelief in Occult Powers.

This has already been noticed, but it may be treated more fully. For three thousand years the Hindus have been vainly seeking to acquire magical powers by "herbs, austerities, and incantations." Two main objects have been the power of transmuting common metals into gold and preparing an elixir which would render men immortal. Every now and then we hear of simpletons who gave their brass vessels to magicians to be changed into gold, with the result of their disappearance. Patanjali enumerates many other magical powers, all of which are as imaginary as alchemy.

Hindus who believe in occult powers are in the mental condition of savages, which is thus described by Lang in *Myth, Ritual, and Religion*:

"They have that nebulous and confused form of mind to which

all things, animate or inanimate, human, animal, vegetable or inorganic, seem on the same level of life, passion and reason. The savage draws no hard and fast line between himself and the things in the world. He regards himself as literally akin to animals and plants, and heavenly bodies, he attributes sex and procreative powers even to stones, and rocks, and he assigns human speech and human feelings to sun and moon, stars and wind, no less than to beasts, birds, and fishes. . . . .

3. Another peculiarity of savage belief naturally connects itself with that which has just been described. The savage has very strong ideas about the persistent existence of the souls of the dead. They retain much of their old nature, but are often more malignant after death than they had been during life. They are frequently at the beck and call of the conjurer, whom they aid with their advice and with their magical power. By virtue of the close connection already spoken of between man and the animals, the souls of the dead are not rarely supposed to migrate into the bodies of beasts, or to resort to the condition of that species of creatures with which each tribe supposes itself to be related by ties of kinship. With the usual inconsistency of mythical belief, the souls of the dead are spoken of, at other times, as if they inhabited a spiritual world, usually a gloomy place which mortal men may visit, but whence no one can escape who has tasted of the food of the ghosts.

4. In connection with spirits a far-reaching savage philosophy prevails. It is not unusual to assign a ghost to all objects, animate or inanimate, and the spirit or strength of a man is frequently regarded as something separable, or something with a definite locality in the body. A man's strength and spirit may reside in his kidney fat, in his heart, in a lock of his hair, or may even be stored by him in some separate receptacle. Very frequently a man is held capable of detaching his soul from his body and, letting it roam about on his business, sometimes in the form of a bird or other animal.

5. Many minor savage beliefs might be named, such as the common faith in friendly or protecting animals, and the notion that 'natural deaths' (as we call them) are always unnatural, that death is always caused by some hostile spirit or conjurer. From this opinion comes the myth that man is not naturally subject to death; that death was somehow introduced into the world by a mistake or misdeed, is a corollary.

6. One more peculiarity of the savage mind remains to be considered in this brief summary. The savage, like the civilised man, is curious. The first faint impulses of the scientific spirit are at work in his brain; he is anxious to give himself an account of the world in which he finds himself. But he is not more curious than he is, on occasion, credulous. His intellect is eager to ask questions, as is the habit of children, but his intellect is also lazy, and he is content with the first answer that comes to hand." Vol. I. pp. 47, 49.

The world of the savage is a jungle of foolish fancies, in which gods and beasts, and men and stars and ghosts all move madly on a level of common personality and animation, all changing shapes at random.

Savages believe in magic and sorcery, Lang says:

"The world and all the things in it being conceived of vaguely as sensible and rational, are supposed to obey the commands of certain members of each tribe, such as chiefs, jugglers, or conjurers. These conjurers can affect the weather, work miracles, assume what shapes, animal, vegetable, or inorganic, they please, and can change other persons into similar shapes. It has already been shown that savage man has regarded all *things* as *persons* much on a level with himself. It has now to be shown *what kind of person he conceives himself to be.* He does not look on men as civilised races regard them, that is, as beings with strict limitations. On the other hand, he thinks of certain members of his tribe as exempt from all limitations, and capable of working every miracle that tradition has ever attributed to prophets or gods. Nor are such miraculous powers supposed by savages to be at all rare among themselves. Though highly valued, miraculous attainments are not believed to be unusual. When a savage regards the sky or sun or wind as a person, he does not mean merely a person with the limitations recognised by civilised races. He means a person with the miraculous powers of the medicine-man.* The sky, sun, wind, or other elemental personage can converse with the dead, and can turn himself and his neighbours into animals, stones and trees.

The savage seeks an explanation, a theory of things based on his experience. But his knowledge of physical causes and of natural laws is exceedingly scanty, and he is driven to fall back upon supernatural explanations. These supernatural causes themselves the savage believes to be matters of experience. It is to his mind a matter of experience that all nature is personal and animated; that men may change shapes with beasts; that incantations and supernatural beings can cause sunshine and storm.

When an untoward event occurs, savages look for its cause among all the less familiar circumstances of the last few days, and select the determining cause very much at random.

In the Pacific Ocean the people of one island always attribute hurricanes to the machinations of the people of the nearest island to windward. The wind comes from them; therefore (as their medicine-men can notoriously influence the weather) they must have sent the wind. This unneighborly act is regarded as a just cause of war. The chief principle, then, of savage science is that antecedence and consequence in time are the same as effect and cause. Again savage science holds that *like effects like;* that you can injure a man, for example, by injuring his effigy. On these principles the savage explains the world to himself, and on those principles he tries to subdue to himself the world. Now the putting of these principles into practice is simply the exercise of art magic, an art to which nothing seems impossible. The belief that medicine-men practise this art is universal among savages.

Any object once in a man's possession, especially his hair or his nails, is supposed to be capable of being used against him by a sorcerer. The part suggests the whole. A lock of a man's hair was part of the man; to destroy the hair is to destroy its former owner.

Among some American Indians, when any is ill, an image of his disease, a boil or what not, is carved in wood. This little image is then

* American Indians call magicians or sorcerers medicine-men. The word medicine here means *mystery*, something wonderful.

placed in a bowl of water and shot at with a gun. The image of the disease being destroyed, the disease itself is expected to disappear.

We found among savages the belief in the power of songs of *incantation* or *mantras*. The most miraculous effects are caused by pronouncing a few lines in rhyme. An American Indian will give a form of incantation with which he says you will be able to call to you all the birds from the sky, and all the foxes and wolves from their burrows. There are supposed to be mantras which raise the wind; which split rocks; by virtue of which the shape of any animal may be assumed at will or a person can fly through the air.

Let us recapitulate the powers attributed all over the people by the lower people to medicine men. The medicine-man has all miracles at his command. He rules the sky, he flies into the air, he becomes visible or invisible at will, he can take and confer any form at pleasure, and resume his human shape. He can control spirits, can converse with the dead, and can descend to their abodes."*

Of all Hindus probably the Shaktas of Bengal have the greatest belief in the ability to acquire occult powers by mantras. Monier Williams quotes the following:

"Holding a scented flower, anointed with sandal, on the left temple, repeat *Om* to the gurus, *Om* to Ganesa, *Om* to Durga. Then with *Om phat*, rub the palms with flowers and clasp the hand thrice over the head, and by snapping the fingers towards ten different directions, secure immunity from the evil spirits."

"Then meditate on the Mátrika, and say, 'Help me, goddess of speech," *am* to the forehead, *ám* to the mouth, *im* to the right eye, *ìm* to the left eye, *um* to the right ear, *úm* to the left ear, *im* to the right cheek, *im* to the left cheek, *rim* to the right nostril, *rím* to the left nostril, *brim* to the right cheek, *brim* to the left cheek, *em* to the upper lip, *aim* to the lower lip, *om* to the upper teeth, *aum* to the lower teeth, *tam, tham, dam, dham*, and *nam* to the several parts of the left leg, *pam* to the right side, *pham* to the left, *bam* to the back, *mam* to the stomach, *yam* to the heart, *ram* to the right shoulder, *lam* to the neck-bone, *ram* to the left shoulder, *sam* from the heart to the right leg, *tram* from the heart to the left leg, *ksham* from the heart to the mouth."†

It is astonishing how any one in his senses can believe in the potency of such nonsense. Along with this proof of a "darkened understanding," among the Vamachara Saktas there is evidence of a "depraved heart." Religion is made an excuse for indulgence in beastly vices. Probably the lowest savages on the face of the earth are not so morally degraded as some Hindu believers in the efficacy of mantras.

Another Hindu belief, equally baseless, is in the *power of austerities*. The sacred books are full of illustrations of their alleged wonders. According to the Ramayana, Ravana passed

* *Myth, Ritual and Religion*, Vol. I. pp. 84, 120 abridged.

† *Brahmanism and Hinduism*; pp. 197, 198.

10,000 years without food. Every year he offered one of his heads to the fire. When about to do so for the tenth time, Brahma appeared, restored all the heads he had lost, made him indestructible to all creatures more powerful than man, with the power of assuming any shape at will. Any person of sense can at once see that all this is a mere invention of the poet.

Many of the Hindu ideals of piety are utterly mistaken. It is a meritorious act to vow not to speak. Some sannyasis wear round their necks an iron frame which is supposed to prevent them from lying down to sleep at ease. Some hang with their heads down, others have their legs up. Some hold up an arm till it is wasted and cannot be bent. A very meritorious act is to sit in the midday sun, with fires blazing all around.

What good is done by such acts? What rewards can be expected from them?

Most men become sannyásis because they are too lazy to work, and can get an easy living by preying upon the industrious. The withered arm, the vow of silence, &c., are merely devices to get more money. Such vows are sins—not acts of merit. Suppose a servant rendered useless some of the tools given to him to work with, would he be praised? God has given us arms to provide food for ourselves, our families and the poor; He has given us the gift of speech that we may comfort the sorrowful, instruct the ignorant. The withered arm and vow of silence defeat those ends. It would be noble for a man to venture into a burning house to rescue children; but it is worse than useless for a man to sit in the middle of blazing fires.

The Hindu belief in the power of mystic syllables or austerities is a mere delusion; but, as will hereafter be explained, by the proper use of the mental powers men may accomplish wonders.

EFFORTS TO ACQUIRE TRUE KNOWLEDGE.

It has been allowed that Ancient India made great advances in Grammar and in Mathematics; that many poetical beauties and excellent moral maxims and sublime descriptions of God may be culled from Sanskrit literature; but the words of Sir H. S. Maine are, on the whole, strictly correct, that it also contains "that which is not true —false morality, false history, false philosophy, false physics." "Greater affinity for eastern thought would be purchased by the sacrifice of that truth, moral, historical, and physical, which will one day bind together the European and Asiatic minds, if ever they are to be united." Macaulay in his celebrated Minute expresses similar opinions: "Medical doctrines, which would disgrace an English farrier,—Astronomy which would move laughter in girls at an English boarding school,—History, abounding with kings thirty feet high, and reigns thirty-thousand years long,— and Geography made up of seas of treacle, and seas of butter."

For thousands of years India has been blindly following false guides; it is time that she opened her eyes and tried to find out the truth. The two chief means to be employed may be briefly stated:

1. **The Cultivation of the Observing Powers.**—It has been mentioned as a characteristic of the Hindu mind to speculate instead of investigate. The result has been false geography, false astronomy, false physiology, &c. Happily there are signs of a better state of things. Professor J. C. Bose has so distinguished himself by careful observation and experiment, as to call forth the admiration of some of the greatest European Scientists. The result is an instalment of the truth, which, in the words of Sir H. S. Maine already quoted, "will bind toether the European and Asiatic minds." It is to be hoped that Professor Bose is only the first of a long line of Indian scientific observers.

2. **The Cultivation of the Critical Faculty.**—Here the Hindu mind has been equally at fault. The most contradictory statements have all been accepted is true; the most improbable legends regarded as genuine history. Illustration has been received as sound logical reasoning. Max Müller, referring to the Brahmanas, of the Vedas, considered to belong to the *Sruti* class of Hindu sacred books, while acknowledging them to contain "no lack of striking thoughts," estimates them as "a literature which for pedantry and absurdity can hardly be matched anywhere . . . These works deserve to be studied as the physician studies the twaddle of idiots, and the raving of madmen."*

The Rev. Dr. K. S. Macdonald, in *The Brahmanas of the Vedas*, quotes the following from the *Satapatha Brahmana*:

"Prajapati beheld all beings in this triple Vedic science. For in it is

* *Ancient Sanskrit Literature.*

the soul of all metres, of all hymns of praise, of all breaths of all the gods. This indeed exists. This is that which is mortal. Prajapati reflected, 'All beings are comprehended in the triple Vedic science: come let me dispose myself in the shape of the triple Vedic science.' He arranged the verses of the Rig-Veda. Twelve-thousand Brihatis, and as many Rik verses which were created by Prajapati, stood in rows in the thirtieth class. Since they stood in the thirtieth class there are thirty nights in the month."

"As a parallel to the above and to much of the reasonings in the Brahmanas, we refer our readers to the pages of *Alice in Wonderland*, and extract the following sample:—

"And how many hours a day did you do lessons?" said Alice to change the subject. "Ten hours the first day," said the Mock Turtle, "nine the next, and so on." "What a curious plan!" exclaimed Alice. "That's the reason they're called lessons" the Gryphon remarked, "because they lessen from day to day. This was quite a new idea to Alice, and she thought it over a little before she made her next remark—"Then the eleventh day must have been a holiday?" "Of course it was," said the Mock Turtle. "And how did you manage on the twelfth?" Alice went on eagerly. "That is enough about lessons," the Gryphon interrupted in a very decided tone, "tell her something about games now."*

According to the above extract from the Satapatha Brahmana, there are thirty nights in the month, because certain verses stood in the thirtieth class! This may well be compared to "the twaddle of idiots." Numberless other illustrations might be given of the same mode of reasoning.

Here happily also a beginning has been made of a more excellent way. There is an admirable lecture by Dr. Bhandarkar of Poona, on *The Critical, Comparative and Historical Method of Inquiry*, explaining the principles on which investigations should be conducted. Like Professor J. C. Bose, Dr. Bhandarkar is also helping to "bind together the European and Asiatic mind," for he is taking part in an *Encyclopædia of Indo-Aryan Research*, to be published in Germany.

By a combination of the two methods, the Indian mind, instead of producing merely "false morality, false history, false philosophy, and false physics" would be adding to the world's stock of true knowledge.

The true Bhakti Yoga.

As already explained, the atheistic system of Kapila had no idea of union with God. Patanjali, to avoid the odium excited by Kapila, brings in Isvara; but practically he is a nonentity. Patanjali, equally with Kapila, ignores the idea of union with God. The latter arose at a subsequent period from the religiousness of the Hindu mind.

---

* *The Brahmanas of the Vedas*, 8vo. 232 pp. 8 As. Post-free, 10 As. Sold by Mr. A. T. Scott, Tract Depôt, Madras.

There is very much to admire in the stages which have been named; as *sálokya*, dwelling in the same abode with God; *sámípya*, nearness to Him; *sárúpya*, assimilation to His likeness; *sáyujya*, union with Him. *Bhakti Yoga*, union with God through love, is another term employed. There is here a seeking after God which is truly noble compared with the system of Patanjali.

But while the *end* is so highly to be praised, the *means* to attain it by Yoga exercises are strongly to be condemned. As already explained, the real effects are to reduce a human being to the condition of a tortoise or hibernating Himalaya marmot; the body is enfeebled by want of exercise; the brain receives only a small supply of impure blood, and the person at last is reduced to a state bordering on idiocy. During all this time he is absolutely useless as a member of society.

Right Conceptions of God.—This lies at the foundation of true religion. There is an Indian proverb, *Yatah devah, tathah bhaktah*, 'As is the god so is the worshipper.' Hinduism generally defines the Supreme Spirit in His nirguna condition, as *sat*, pure existence, as opposed to non-existence; *cit*, pure thought in the negation of non-thought; *ananda*, pure bliss in freedom from the miseries of life and transmigration."*

Brahma, in his *nirguna* condition, is supposed to be like a Hindu raja who spends his life in sloth within his palace, heedless of what is going on throughout his dominions, and leaving everything to his ministers.

"Unencumbered by the cares of empire," says Dr. Duff, "or the functions of a superintending providence, he effectuates no good, inflicts no evil, suffers no pain. He exists in a state of undisturbed repose—a sleep so deep as never to be disturbed by a dream—even without any consciousness of his own existence."

The three qualities which Brahma, in his *saguna* state, possesses are *sattva*, truth, *rajas*, passion, a longing for worldly pleasure, and *tamas*, darkness. Prahláda is represented, in the Vishnu Purana, as thus addressing Vishnu: "Thou art knowledge and ignorance, truth and falsehood, poison and ambrosia."

Hinduism has no correct idea of holiness. Brahma, Vishnu, and Siva, are nowhere regarded in the Sastras as holy beings. On the contrary, they are all described as stained with great crimes. The gods of Hinduism act like Indian rajas, contending with each other for power, each favouring his own party, and indulging in every vice or committing any crime his evil heart may desire. The Hindu gods reflect the national character. By contemplating them and their actions, worshippers are made worse instead of better.

Christianity, on the other hand, gives the most exalted ideas of God, and His worship is fitted to have a most beneficial influence.

---

* Monier Williams, *Hinduism and Brahmanism*, pp. 34, 35.

He is the "I AM," the Self-existent, "without beginning of days or end of years." "From everlasting to everlasting, Thou art God." He is unchanging, "the same yesterday, and to-day, and for ever." He is the Almighty God. He called the universe into existence, and His government extends over all. He is never unconscious. He never slumbers nor sleeps. "The Creator of the ends of the earth fainteth not, neither is weary." He knows everything that takes place throughout His vast dominions. Not a hair of our head can fall to the ground without His knowledge; every thought of our heart is known to Him. His ear is ever open to the cry of His children.

The one true God is most unlike ths *saguna* Brahma. He is a God of truth; He is light, and in Him is no darkness at all. His most glorious attribute is His spotless holiness. Sin is that abominable thing which He hates. "Holy, holy, holy is the Lord God of hosts." Instead of exhibiting, like Brahma, an example of selfishness, He is continually doing good to His creatures. His character is expressed in one word—God is LOVE. Still, it is not the feeling which looks upon good and evil with equal eye. If a king allowed crime to be unpunished, his kingdom would become like a hell. But God's own declaration is, "As I live, saith the Lord God, I have no pleasure in the death of the wicked; but that the wicked turn from his evil way and live."

Milton thus describes the feelings which ought to arise in the mind from the contemplation of the earth and heavens:

> "These are thy glorious works, Parent of good,
> Almighty, thine this universal frame,
> Thus wondrous fair; thyself how wondrous then!
> Unspeakable, who sitt'st above these heavens,
> To us invisible or dimly seen
> In these thy lowest works; yet these declare
> Thy goodness beyond thought, and power Divine."

This great Being deserves our worship. He first called us into existence; we are dependent upon Him for every breath that we draw; we live upon His earth; everything we possess is His gift. He is both our Father in heaven and our King, deserving our warmest love and utmost respect. To worship Him is both our duty, and would have an excellent influence upon our character.

Confession of Sin the first step to Bhakti Yoga.—Suppose children have been grossly ungrateful and disobedient to a kind father, they cannot go to him simply expressing their love. Indeed, when children feel that they have done wrong, they shun the presence of their father.

The belief is universal that man is a sinner,* and deserves

---

* Its denial by Swami Vivekananda shows how ignorant he is of his own heart, and his unfitness to be a religious teacher.

punishment. How to be delivered from its penalty is the grand inquiry.

Hinduism gives contradictory answers whether sin can be forgiven or not. One doctrine is that the fruit of every action, good are bad, must be reaped. The other is that the most worthless means suffice for the removal of sin. Almsgiving, pilgrimages, bathing in supposed sacred waters, are some of the ways prescribed. Drinking water in which a Brahman has dipt his toe, or repeating the name of Hari, is supposed to absolve from the greatest crimes.

The holiest men are the first to admit their own sinfulness. Most people compare themselves with their neighbours, and are satisfied if they come up to their standard. Sometimes they contrast themselves with persons notoriously wicked, and are proud because they think themselves better. Truly good men compare themselves with what God's law requires, and their confession is, "We are all as an unclean thing, and all our righteousnesses are as filthy rags."

The two great sins chargeable against every human being are *ungodliness* and *selfishness.*

The verdict pronounced upon Belshazzar, king of Babylon, was: "Thou art weighed in the balances, and art found wanting." The prophet Daniel explained the grounds of this judgment when he said, "The God in whose hand thy breath is, and whose are all thy ways, hast thou not glorified." When conscience awakes, we see nothing in the past but a career of guilt—the grand purpose of our lives neglected, the great God treated with indifference, His holy law trampled under foot. God contrasts the gratitude of the very beasts with the regardlessness of man. "I have nourished and brought up children, and they have rebelled against me. The ox knoweth his owner and the ass his master's crib; but Israel doth not know, my people doth not consider."

Need of an Incarnation.—In all ages the hope has been more or less entertained that God would become incarnate to deliver man from the burden of sin and misery under which the world is groaning. Hinduism has its incarnations. The Kalki Avatar is yet to come, when Vishnu, at the end of the Kali Yug, is to appear seated on a white horse, with drawn sword in his hand blazing like a comet, for the destruction of the wicked, and the restoration of purity.

Christianity also teaches that man is so deeply plunged in sin and his guilt is so great, that a Divine incarnation was necessary for his deliverance. The first promise of this was given by God Himself thousands of years ago. The Son of God, pitying the human race, came down from heaven for our salvation. By His death on the cross He bore the punishment due to our sins; by His obedience to the law of God He wrought out a perfect righteousness, which, like a spotless robe, is given to His followers.

A very erroneous impression prevails among some Hindus. They think that Christianity represents God as angry till propitiated by the Son. On the contrary, the atonement originated in the love of the Father. "God so loved the world that He gave His only begotten Son" to be our Saviour. But the Son was equally willing. His response was, "Lo! I come; I delight to do Thy will."

Some think that God may freely pardon sin without an atonement. But God is our King as well as our Father, and to forgive sin without satisfaction to justice, would tend to spread rebellion throughout the universe.

The following illustration has been used: A part of the army of one of the wisest and best of kings conspired against him. They were seized, disarmed, and condemned to die. The king wished to save their lives, but a free pardon would have tempted others to rebel. The king's only son, who was commander-in-chief of the army, also wished to deliver the condemned men. It was agreed that the prince should suffer punishment in their stead, and when this was done, those who asked pardon in his name would be forgiven.

As the king's son in the parable offered to suffer that the rebel soldiers might be spared, so the eternal Son of God agreed to become man as the Lord Jesus Christ, to suffer and die in our stead. For 33 years He lived on earth, perfectly obeying all God's laws, and at last died on the cross. On the third day He rose from the dead, and afterwards ascended to heaven, where He occupies the highest place of honour. Pardon is now freely offered to all who seek it in His name, accepting Him as their Saviour.

No illustration that can be given fully meets the case; but the foregoing may give some idea of the way in which God's justice and mercy are reconciled through Christianity.

The stages mentioned in Hindu sacred books will now be considered, pointing out the qualifications necessary.

Salokya.—This denotes dwelling in the same world with God. Such is the case, even here. We are continually in God's presence. A holy man of old said:

"O Lord thou hast searched me and known me. Thou knowest my downsitting and mine uprising, Thou understandest my thought afar off. Thou compassest my path and my lying down, and art acquainted with all my ways. For there is not a word in my tongue, but, lo, O Lord, Thou knowest it altogether. Thou hast beset me behind and before, and laid thine hand upon me. Such knowledge is too wonderful for me; it is high, I cannot attain unto it. Whither shall I go from thy spirit, or whither shall I flee from thy presence? If I ascend up into heaven Thou art there; if I make my bed in Sheol,* behold Thou art there. If I take the wings of the morning, and dwell in the uttermost parts of the sea; even there shall thy hand lead me, and thy right hand shall hold

* The grave; the unseen world.

me. If I say, surely the darkness shall cover me; even the night shall be light about me. Yea, the darkness hideth not from Thee; but the night shineth as the day; the darkness and the light are both alike to Thee."—*Psalm* 139. 1-12.

But although we are thus continually in God's presence, and indebted to Him for every breath we draw, the great majority of men never think of Him, ignore His existence, and if His name is mentioned, it is only an idle exclamation.

There have, however, been a few who have felt that God is ever with them. It is said of a good man, in very early times, called Enoch, that he "walked with God." He lived as if God were by his side. Another good man said, "I am continually with Thee." We live in God's world. Of the objects around us, we may say, "My Father made them all." We should constantly realize God's presence. This is the true *Sálokya,* begun on earth and continued in heaven.

Samipya, nearness to God.—This denotes increasing love and admiration, accompanied by a desire for closer intercourse, like the warmest feeling between father and son. The child says, "My father." The reply is, "Son, thou art ever with me." The son delights in his father's presence; he tells him all his joys and sorrows; he constantly seeks his help and guidance. Tennyson says:

> "Speak, thou, to Him for He hears, and spirit with Spirit may meet,
> Closer is He than breathing, nearer than hands and feet."

Sarupya, assimilation to God's likeness. This does not refer to His bodily form, for He has none; but to His character. A child naturally imitates his father in disposition and conduct. The Lord Jesus Christ holds up our heavenly Father as our model. "Be ye perfect even as your Father in heaven is perfect." This Jesus Christ explained by His own conduct, "leaving us an example that we should follow His steps."

To overcome sin and become like God, we need Divine help. Here the Christian doctrine of the Trinity is felt to be adapted to our needs. Although Christians firmly hold God's unity, yet in some mysterious way there is a Father, Son, and Holy Spirit, who all unite for man's redemption. The peculiar office of the Holy Spirit is to sanctify, to enable us to overcome sin, and to be adorned with all the beauties of holiness. His help is given in answer to prayer. The promise is, "If ye being evil know how to give good gifts unto your children; how much more shall your heavenly Father give the Holy Spirit to them that ask Him?"

Besides prayer for the Holy Spirit, there must be watchfulness against sin, avoidance of temptation, study of the scriptures and other good books, observance of the Lord's day, attendance at public worship, association with good men, etc.

The Lord Jesus Christ thus summed up our duty:

1. Thou shalt love the Lord thy God with all thy heart.
2. Thou shalt love thy neighbour as thyself.

True *bhakti yoga* includes both. A man is not to be selfishly employed in what he considers love to God, while he has no regard for his fellow men. What would be thought of a child who loved his father, but heeded not his brothers and sisters? Would his father be pleased with that love? It is said of God, "Thou art good and doest good." If we would be truly like God, we must love all around us and seek their benefit. Without this, our religion is vain, and pure selfishness.

Sayujya.—This is commonly understood as meaning absorption into the Supreme Spirit. The illustrations, a river emptying itself into the ocean or a drop uniting with the ocean, are accepted as proofs. The hollowness of such reasoning has already been shown. Another illustration proves the contrary; as oil and water cannot unite, so the soul cannot be absorbed in God.

The doctrine of absorption is a mere Vedantist figment. Starting with the other figments that there is only one existence and that the soul is eternal, this theory was invented as well as the blasphemous assertions, *Brahmásmi, Tat twam asi,* I am Brahma, That thou art.

The Rev. Lal Behari Day has the following remarks on absorption:

"Such a doctrine, to say the least, is highly improbable; for it is only homogeneous (of the same kind) substances that mix. But God is unique in the universe; there is none like Him. How then can any other being be absorbed in him? Again, it is doubtful whether absorption into the divine essence is a source of happiness to a creature. For absorption into the divine essence implies a loss of the sense of personal identity, that is, annihilation. And how can a creature that is annihilated be happy!"*

The only happiness is release from the supposed eternal weary round of transmigration.

The Creator and the creature must for ever remain distinct. The Visishtadwaitas deny that Jiva becomes absolutely united with Parabrahmam, and Christianity does the same. But there may be the closest union. The apostle Paul says of true Christians, "Know ye not that ye are the temple of God, and that the Spirit of God dwelleth in you." Paul himself was so full of love to Christ that he said, "I live; yet not I, but Christ liveth in me." This union, begun on earth, becomes still closer in heaven. It is a state of conscious happy existence in God's presence, never to have an end. What a glorious prospect! How well worthy of our most strenuous efforts to attain it!

---

* *On Vedantism.*

CONCLUDING APPEAL.

'The old order changeth yielding place to new.'

Causes of the failure of Hindu Philosophers.—The late Dr. Krishna Mohun Banerjea, Sanskrit Examiner to the Calcutta University, has the following remarks on this point:—

"They propounded many theories on the origin of the world, the nature of God, the properties of matter and mind."

"Sciences, distinct in themselves, were blended together. Objects which surpassed the limits of the human understanding, were pursued with the same confidence and eagerness with which the easiest questions were investigated. The philosophers professed to have solved problems, really out of the range of our knowledge, while they threw doubts on matters which everybody believed, and which none could deny without belying his nature.

"The authors (of systems) began to dogmatize in the very infancy of philosophical speculation. They drew general conclusions before they had collected facts. They worked up their own ideas, without sufficient attention to external phenomena.

"Neither did they stop to consider the true range of human capacity, and the limits which mark off things *comprehensible*, from those that are incomprehensible. While they boldly speculated on points which man can never determine by the exercise of reason, they did not deal fairly with those inquiries for which they were really competent. No wonder that their researches were unsatisfactory."*

It was the same in ancient Europe. Macaulay, in his Essay on Bacon and the Stoical Philosophy, says:

"Words and more words, and nothing but words, had been all the fruit of all the toil of all the most renowned sages of sixty generations. The ancient philosophers promised what was impracticable; they despised what was practicable; they filled the world with long words and long beards; and they left it as wicked and ignorant as they found it."

False Beliefs to be abandoned.—For three thousand years falsehood has reigned supreme in India. In the words of Sir H. S. Maine, Oriental Culture has been "false morality, false history, false philosophy, and false physics." Its social system of caste, the distinguishing feature of Hinduism, is based on a blasphemous lie. Manu's Code, the highest Hindu legal authority, makes the following statements:

93. Since he sprang from the most excellent part, since he was the first-born, and since he holds the Vedas, the Brahman is, by right, the lord of all this creation. Book I.

413. But a Sudra, whether bought or not bought, (the Brahman) may compel to practise servitude; for that (Sudra) was created by the Self-existent merely for the service of the Brahman. VIII.

---

* *Dialogues on Hindu Philosophy*, pp. 71, 72. Abridged.

80. One may not give advice to a Sudra, nor (give him) the remains (of food) or (of) butter that has been offered. And one may not teach him the law or enjoin upon him (religious) observances. IV.

Sir H. S. Maine calls caste, "The most disastrous and blighting of human institutions:"* "The system of caste," says Principal Caird, "involves the worst of all wrongs to humanity, that of hallowing evil by the authority and sanction of religion. Instead of breaking down artificial barriers, waging war with false separations, softening divisions and undermining class hatreds and antipathies, religion becomes itself the very consecration of them."

Yet to this false system have Hindus clung with a tenacity dearer than life.

Saddest of all, unnumbered generations have gone down to death with a lie in their right hand, trusting for salvation to false promises. The sacred books of the Hindus are full of such. The first chapter of Valmiki's Ramayana concludes as follows:

"He that readeth this sacred, sin-destroying, merit-bestowing history of Rama, like unto the Veda itself, becometh cleansed from all sin. And the man that readeth this Ramayana, conferring length of days, after death is honoured in heaven, along with his sons, grandsons, and relations."†

The following specimens are from the Vishnu Purana:

"Whoever listens to the history of Prahlada is immediately cleansed from all his sins." Book I. Chapter 20.

"This sacred stream (the Ganges) heard of, desired, seen, touched, bathed in, or hymned, day by day, sanctifies all beings; and those who even at a distance of a hundred yojanas, exclaim, Ganga, Ganga, atone for the sins committed during their previous lives." Book II. Chapter 8.

God said of the Jews in ancient times, "The prophets prophesy falsely and priests bear rule by their means, and my people *love to have it so*." The same may be said, alas! of Hindus.

The immediate subject of remarks is the Yoga Sutras of Patanjali. It has been shown that the course recommended is selfish, delusive, and pernicious. The same remark applies in some measure to the Bhagavad Gita, where Yoga exercises are encouraged. Book IV. says:

27. "The *muni* who excludeth (from his mind) external objects, (concentrating) the visual power between the brows, and making the upward and downward life-breaths, ever sending both through the nostrils, who restraineth the senses, mind and understanding, intent on final emancipation, from whom desire, fear, and wrath have departed, is indeed for ever free (from birth and death)."

Let the belief in the power of "austerities and incantations" be abandoned. Such ideas are worthy only of children and savages. Let them rather imitate the men, who, by a wise use of

* *Ancient Law.* † Translation by Manmatha Nath Dutt, M. A.

the faculties which God had given them, devised means by which thousands of people may travel with ease at the rate of 40 miles an hour, by which the sun is made to paint pictures, and lightning to convey messages.

"Awakened India," instead of adopting the fowl or tortoise upset posture, with his eye fixed on the tip of his nose and seeking "the suppression of the transformations of the thinking principle", should rather endeavour to have his muscles braced like those of Prince Ranjitsinhji, his faculties of observation cultivated like those of Professor Bose, his ability to weigh evidence developed like that of Dr. Bhandarkar. Instead of a dreamy pessimism, let there be active benevolence. Thus would India advance in civilization with a speed before unknown.

Above all, let the deep religious feeling of the Hindu mind be wisely directed. Let the *Bhakti Yoga* have for its object the loftiest ideal of majesty, wisdom, goodness, and purity. Such is the great Creator and Lord of the Universe. We should aim at living as continually in His presence; we should realize His nearness to us; we should strive to be like Him; we should seek to have Him dwelling in our hearts as in a temple, looking forward to the time when we shall see Him face to face in His Kingdom above.

One of the worst features of the time is the hypocrisy prevalent among many educated Hindus from a feeling of false patriotism. *The Hindu*, a Madras journal, says:

"We have observed of late a tendency on the part of some of our educated countrymen to apply their mental powers for irrationally reactionary purposes. Social customs and institutions which are evil in their results, and are the product of past simpler and less civilized conditions, have received elaborate defence; and even certain merits have been attached to them.

"They defend every superstition of our people; they believe in every dogma and worthless ceremonial, and are generally slaves of our exacting priesthood. In their judgment, nothing that our ancestors did could be wrong. Everything Indian is excellent itself, and everything foreign the opposite."

Principal Wordsworth made the same complaint with regard to educated men in Bombay:

"I find some of them employing all the resources of theological sophistry and cant, not simply to palliate, but to vindicate what is plainly one of the most cruel, blighting, and selfish forms of human superstition and tyranny. I find others manœuvring to arrest every sincere effort at reform, sophisticating between right and wrong, defaming the character and motives of reformers."

Of all false patriotism that is the worst which seeks by sophistry to defend erroneous beliefs because they are national. It promotes hypocrisy and disregard of truth among its advocates, while it is a grievous wrong to their ignorant countrymen, tending to perpetuate the reign of error and superstition. Truthfulness lies at the basis of every virtuous character, and patriotism resting on hypocrisy is a mere sham.

Keshub Chunder Sen justly says:

"In science there cannot be sects or divisions, schisms or enmities. Is there one astronomy for the East and another for the West? Is there an Asiatic optics as distinguished from European optics? Science is one. It is one yesterday to-day and for ever; the same in the East and the West; it recognises neither caste, nor colour, nor nationality. It is God's science, the eternal verity of things."

It is the same in religion.

If each country had its own God, there might be different religions; but all intelligent men are now agreed that there is only one God, the Creator, Preserver, and Governor of the Universe. The Brotherhood of Man is similarly acknowledged.

"Children we are all
One great Father, in whatever clime,
His providence hath cast the seed of life;
All tongues, all colours."

Since God is one and all men are alike His children, it is reasonable to suppose that He has given only one religion, as there is only one science.

The most enlightened countries in Europe and America have embraced a religion first made known to them by Asiatics, and did not reject it from false patriotism, saying, "We must have national religions." A true patriot accepts truth from any quarter.

The remark of the late Sir Madava Row should be deeply impressed upon educated Hindus: **What is not TRUE, is not PATRIOTIC.**

Let this be our prayer with regard to India:

"O Father, touch the East, with light,
The light that shone when Hope was born."

Happily there are some signs of the dawn, and the sky will redden more and more unto the perfect day. Pessimism and falsehood of every kind will yet vanish before its rays. Instead of accepting this as the Kali Yuga, let us make strenuous efforts that it may become the Krita or Satya Yuga.

"Ring out the old, ring in the new,
Ring out the false, ring in the true.

Ring in the valiant man and free,
The larger heart, the kindlier hand;
Ring out the darkness of the land,
Ring in the Christ that is to be."

- *Tennyson.*

APPENDIX.

REMARKS

ON

"YOGA PHILOSOPHY:

"Lectures delivered in New York, 1895-96, by the Swami Vivekananda on Raja Yoga; also Patanjali's Yoga Aphorisms, with Commentaries."

Dean Farrar says of the present day:

"Every variety of blasphemy and folly has its apostles. Every negation, however audacious and desolating, has its defenders on the platform and press. Every superstition, however grotesque and discredited, has its fanatical partisans and devotees."

An illustration of this is afforded by the addresses of Swami Vivekananda and his work above-mentioned.

Babu Norendra Nath Dutt, who has assumed the title of Swami Vivekananda (bliss discrimination), belongs to a well-known Calcutta family, some of whose members are Christians. He was a student in the General Assembly's Institution, and at the age of 21 took the B. A. Degree in 1884, in the second class. His father was a lawyer, and he himself studied law with a view to practise; but he relinquished his design. *The Indian Mirror* says: "He used to attend divine services held in the Brahmo churches, and was one of the actors on the stage which was erected at the house of the late Babu Keshab Chunder Sen to represent a religious drama." He also sang hymns in one of the Brahmo Samajes of Calcutta; but he was especially influenced by the Paramahansa Ramkrishna.

A sannyasi of the old type is a supposed abandoner of worldly concerns, who lives an ascetic life. Norendra Dath Dutt founded a new order, wearing "gorgeous" silk robes and living in "first class" American hotels. His outlandish dress, Bengali fluency, and command of English, excited considerable attention, especially among ladies in America.

Some points in the Swami's Lectures and *Yoga Philosophy* will now be noticed.

Evolution of God.—The Swami, during his travels, heard something about Darwin's theory of evolution. In his *Yoga Philosophy* he thus impiously applies it to the Deity:

"Starting from some fungus, some very minute, microscopic bubble, and all the time drawing from that infinite storehouse of energy, the form is changed slowly and slowly, until, in course of time it becomes a plant, then an animal, then man, ultimately God." Page 43.

Denial of Sin.—At Chicago the Swami said :

"Ye are the children of God, the sharers of immortal bliss, holy and perfect beings. Ye, divinities on earth, sinners ! It is a sin to call a man so. It is a standing libel on human nature."

This is repeated in a New York lecture, quoted in *The Brahmavadin,* August 29, 1896 :

"The worst lie that you ever told yourself was that you were a sinner, or a wicked man."

The very reverse is the case. The worst lie that you ever told yourself is that you are *not* a sinner. Who can truthfully say that he has never spoken a lie or angry word, that he has never given way to envious, lustful thoughts ?

Nearly the whole human race, with one voice, acknowledge themselves to be sinners. Why do Hindus bathe in the Ganges and other supposed sacred waters except to wash away sin ?

It is only pride and ignorance that make a man deny that he is a sinner. The holiest men are the first to acknowledge it. Some Brahmans daily make this acknowledgment :—

Pápo'ham pápakarmáham pápátma pápasambhava.

"I am sin ; I commit sin : my soul is sinful ; I am conceived in sin."

The first step in true religion is the heartfelt confession to God, "Father, I have sinned, and am no more worthy to be called Thy son." The Rev. F. W. Kellett, M.A., in a paper entitled, *The Sense of Sin in the Light of History,** shows that "the deeper the sense of sin, the truer the religion." The poor peasant who can only humbly cry, 'God be merciful to me a sinner,' knows far more of true religion than the Swami.

Blasphemous Claim to Divinity.—In the New York lecture quoted in *the Brahmavadin,* August 29th 1896, the Swami says :—

"It is the greatest of all lies that we are men ; we are the god of the universe. We have been always worshipping our own selves.

"Thou art that (*tat twam asi.*) And the whole universe of myriads of suns and moons everything that speaks, with one voice will say, 'Thou art that.' "†

Such assertions can only be compared to the ravings of a madman in a lunatic asylum, who fancies himself a king. They are thus exposed : Gaudapurnananda says :—

* Sold by Mr. A. T. Scott, Tract Depot, Madras. Price ¼ Anna.

† *The Brahmavadin* (Oct. 12, 1895, p. 30) makes the same claim in terms equally objectionable. "Man is not the mere creature of a God; he is God himself. He has not simply the image impressed upon him of his Creator. He is himself the Creator."

"Thou art verily rifled, O thou animal soul, of thy understanding, by this dark theory of Maya, because like a maniac, thou constantly ravest, 'I am Brahma.' Where is thy divinity, thy sovereignty, thy omniscience? Oh thou animal soul! thou art as different from Brahma as is a mustard seed from Mount Meru. Thou art a finite soul, He is infinite. Thou canst occupy but one space at a time, He is always everywhere. Thou art momentarily happy or miserable, He is happy at all times. How canst thou say 'I am He?' Hast thou no shame?"‡

Ramanuja, another celebrated Hindu writer, argues against it similarly:—

"The word *tat* (it) stands for the ocean of immortality, full of supreme felicity. The word *twam* (thou) stands for a miserable person, distracted through fear of the world. The two cannot therefore be one. They are substantially different. He is to be worshipped by the whole world. Thou art but His slave. How could there be an image or inflection of the infinite and spotless One? There may be a reflection of a finite substance; how could there be such a thing of the Infinite? How canst thou, oh slow of thought! say, I am He, who has set up this immense sphere of the universe in its fulness? By the mercy of the Most High a little understanding has been committed to thee: it is not for thee, oh perverse one, to say, therefore I am God."*

Any one who believes the above assertions of the Swami must be a fellow-lunatic. The conscience of every sane, thoughtful man must tell him that he has sinned both in thought, word, and deed, and that he has no claim to divinity.

Equal Acceptance of Truth and Falsehood.—In the Vishnu Purana, Prahláda thus addresses Vishnu: "Thou art knowledge and ignorance; thou art truth and untruth; thou art poison and nectar."† The same words may be applied to the Swami and to his guru Ramkrishna.

Hindus constantly mistake illustration for argument. Because a rope may be mistaken for a snake, therefore the universe is unreal. In *The Nineteenth Century* for August, Max Müller quotes some of the "Precepts of Ramkrishna Paramahansa." The following is an example:—

"(11.) As one can ascend to the top of a house by means of a ladder, or a bamboo, or a staircase, or a rope, so diverse are the ways and means to approach God, and every religion in the world shows one of these ways."

This is a mere variation of the well-known saying, "As there are several roads to the same city, so all religions lead to God."

---

* Banerjea's *Dialogues on Hindu Philosophy*, pp. 379, 408.

† Manmatha Nath Dutt's Translation, p. 99.

As well might it be said to a traveller, "Take any railroad; they all lead to the same city."

Ramkrishna's argument amounts to this, "As there are several ways of getting to the top of a house, so the most contradictory statements are all true.' The logic of this is worthless.

The Indian Nation thus notices ideas like the above propounded by the Swami at the Parliament of Religions:

"It is useless speaking of the conflicting doctrines as different paths leading to a 'common goal.' We should very much like to know what this common centre is, for we must confess we can conceive of none which can be reached by theism and atheism alike. We are past that stage when a mere phrase would charm us into slavery, and until more light dawns upon us we must hold 'common centre' and 'convergence of diverging radii' to be mere phrases." April 9th, 1894.

Veiled Atheism and Sneer at Prayer.—"Surface scientists" are said to be

"More culpable than those who think their prayers are answered by a being or beings, above the clouds, or than those who believe that their petitions will make such beings change the course of the universe." Preface, p. viii.

Raja Yoga teaches:

"That desires and wants are in man, that the power of supply is also in man; and that wherever and whenever a desire, a want, a prayer, has been fulfilled, it was out of this infinite magazine that the supply came, and not from any supernatural being. The idea of supernatural beings may rouse to a certain extent the power of action in man, but it also brings spiritual decay. It brings dependence; it brings fears, it brings superstition. It degenerates into a horrible belief in the natural weakness of man. There is no supernatural, says the Yogi." pp. viii. ix.

"The man who thinks that he is receiving responses to his prayers does not know that the fulfilment came only from his own nature, that he has succeeded by the mental attitude of prayer in waking up a bit of this infinite power which is coiled up within himself. Whom thus, men ignorantly worship under various names, through fear and tribulation, the Yogi declares to the world to be the real power coiled up in every being, the mother of eternal happiness, if we know how to approach her. And Raja Yoga is the science of religion, the rationale of all worship, all prayers, forms, ceremonies, and miracles." p. 55.

Polytheism:—

"Even the Devas (gods) will have to come down again, and attain to salvation through a human body." p. 24.

Akasa.

The Swami admits that the whole of Raja Yoga is based on the Sânkhya Philosophy. (p. 13.) It has been shown (see page 2) that Kapila makes Akása only one of the five grosser elements (mahábúta), with sound as its distinguishing property, and the ear as its organ. In spite of this the Swami make *ákása,* instead of *Prakriti*: the source of all things. The Bhagavad Gita agrees with the Sânkhya:

"Under my supervision Prakriti produceth both the movable and the immovable. It is in this way, O Arjuna, that the universe revolveth." ix. 10.

Dr. Bhandarkar writes:*

"Some of the Upanishads mention ákása as the immediate product of the primeval A'tmá and from ákása is produced, they say, the air (Váyu), from the air, fire (Agni), from fire, water, from water, earth, from earth, herbs, &c. In one Upanishad, the Chhándogya, ákása is spoken as the creator of names and forms and the Scholiasts identify this ákása with Brahman. According to the Yoga Philosophy, of the two principles as the constituents of the universe, the second principle should certainly be Prakriti and not ákása."

PRANA AND ITS MAGICAL POWERS.

Mrs. Besant lately made herself ridiculous by her lecture at Lahore on "Western Science justifying Eastern Occultism," in which she said that the Ganges and idols owed their virtue to being magnetised by Rishis! The Swami has made a somewhat similar attempt to justify his assertion at Chicago, that "the latest discoveries of science seem like echoes of the high spiritual flights of Vedantic Philosophy."

Professor Venis, of Benares, writes:† "In the Sánkhya and Yoga systems, the term prána does not seem to have denoted more than *breath* or principle of life."‡ At pp. 13, 14, of this pamphlet, the Sutras of Patanjali on the subject are given as translated by Mr. Manilal Nabhubhai Dvivedi, with his explanation. *Pránáyáma* is defined "as the control of the breath." The Swami had heard something of "cosmic energy"; so he identifies it with *prána,* and endows it with magical powers.

In the Glossary *Prána* is defined as, "The sum-total of the cosmic energy; the vital forces in the body." (p. 232.)

Pránáyáma is thus explained:

"*Pránáyáma* is not, as many think, something about the breath; breath, indeed, has very little to do with it, if anything. Breathing is only one of the many exercises though which we get to the real Pránáyáma. Pránáyáma means the control of Prána." p. 30.

Although 'breathing' is thus depreciated, with the flat contradiction which does not trouble Hindu philosophers, it is elsewhere stated to be the means of attaining tremendous powers:

---

* Letter to the writer, November 18th, 1896.

† Letter, dated December 26th, 1896.

‡ Prána sometimes denotes Brahman, the Supreme Spirit, but not in the Sánkhya.

"Now we shall see why breathing is practised. In the first place from rhythmical breathing will come a tendency of all the molecules in the body to have the same direction. When mind changes into will, the currents change into a motion similar to electricity, because the nerves have been proved to show polarity under action of electric currents. This shows that when the will evolves into the nerve currents it is changed into something like electricity. When all the motions of the body have become perfectly rhythmical the body has, as it were, become a gigantic battery of will. This tremendous will is exactly what the Yogí wants. This is, therefore, a physiological explanation of the breathing exercise. It tends to bring a rhythmic action in the body, and helps us, through the respirating centre, to control the other centres. The aim of Pránáyáma here is to rouse the coiled-up power in the Múládhára, called the Kundaliní." pp. 50, 51.

Professor Bose and every scientist will characterise the foregoing as simply *balderdash*.

The following are some of the marvellous powers said to be acquired by Pránáyáma:

1. **Control of the Universe.**

"Pránáyáma opens to us the door to almost unlimited power. Suppose for instance one understood the Prána perfectly, and could control it, what power on earth could there be that would not be his? He would be able to move the sun and stars out of their places, to control everything in the universe, from the atoms to the biggest suns, because he could control the Prána. This is the end and aim of Pránáyáma. When the Yogí becomes perfect there will be nothing in nature not under his control. If he orders the gods to come, they will come at his bidding; if he asks the departed to come, they will come at his bidding." p. 32.

2. **Freedom from Sickness and Misery.**

"Every part of the body can be filled with Prána, this vital force, and when you are able to do that, you can control the whole body. All the sickness and misery felt in the body will be perfectly controlled, and not only so, you will be able to control another's body." p. 39.

3. **Ability to enter another's body.**—It is thus explained:

"The Yogi can enter a dead body and make it get up and move, even when he himself is working in another body." p. 198.

The Swami gives a list of other wonderful powers which may be acquired.

Every sensible man will regard the foregoing claims as only the ravings of a lunatic. Hindus, with boundless credulity, may accept them, but this only shows how their intellectual powers have been dwarfed by their creed.

Belief in the power of Mantras.—The Swami says:

"The power of words. There are certain sacred words, called mantrams, which have power, when repeated under certain conditions, to produce these extraordinary powers. We are living in the midst of

such a mass of miracles, day and night, that we do not think anything of them. There is no limit to man's power, the power of words, and the power of mind." p. 208.

It has been shown that such superstitious beliefs belong to savages. (See pp. 43-46) No mantra can kill or cure even a fly.

A person who can believe that the universe had no intelligent Author can believe anything. Lecky, in his *History of European Morals*, says that about the beginning of the Christian era:

"The notions, too, of magic and astrology, were detached from all theological belief, and might be found among many who were absolute atheists." Vol. I. p. 393.

It has been shown that belief in Yoga powers is all a delusion, and that, as Barth says, the exercises, "**conscientiously observed, can only issue in folly and idiocy.**"

Colonel Olcott came to India a believer in the occult powers of Yogis. In his search for them he found only "a crowd of painted impostors who masquerade as *Sadhus*, to cheat the charitable, and secretly give loose to their beastly nature."*

The Swami says in the summary prefixed to his Yoga Philosophy:

"Be free. This is the whole of religion."

There is another definition of religion, given by the great Teacher, which the reader is asked to ponder:

"*Thou shalt love the Lord thy God with all thy heart, and with all thy soul, and with all thy strength, and with all thy mind; and thy neighbour as thyself.*"

To do this we need Divine help, which will be given in answer to earnest prayer.

---

* Addresses, p. 184.

ENGLISH PUBLICATIONS FOR INDIAN READERS.

SOCIAL REFORM.

On Decision of Character and Moral Courage. 8vo. 56 pp. 1½ As. Post-free, 2 As.

A reprint of Foster's Celebrated Essay, with some remarks on its application to India.

Sanitary Reform in India. 55 pp. 2 As. Post-free, 2½ As.

How lakhs of Lives may be saved every year, and crores of cases of Sickness prevented; Precautions against Fever, Cholera, Diabetes, &c.

Is India Becoming Poorer or Richer? With Remedies for the Existing Poverty. 8vo. 82 pp. 2½ As. Post-free, 3 As.

The prevailing idea with regard to the increasing poverty of India shown to be incorrect, and the true means of promoting its wealth explained.

Debt and the Right Use of Money. 8vo. 32 pp. 1 Anna.

Prevalence of Debt in India; its Causes; Evils; how to get out of it; with Franklin's Way to Wealth, &c.

Purity Reform. 8vo. 32 pp. 1 Anna.

The great need of this reform shown, and the means for its promotion.

Temperance Reform in India. 8vo. 40 pp. 1½ As. Post-free, 2 As.

Intoxicating liquors in Ancient India; Intemperance in England; Temperance Reform in the West; spread of Intemperance in India; Temperance Reform in India; how to promote Temperance Reform; with Portraits of Livesey, Father Mathew, Sir Wilfred Lawson, Dean Farrar, Messrs. Samuel Smith and Caine.

Caste. 8vo. 66 pp. 2 As. Post-free, 2½ As.

Supposed and real origin of Caste; Laws of Caste according to Manu; its Effects; Duty with regard to it.

The Women of India and What can be Done for Them. 8vo. 158 pp. 4 As. Post-free, 5½ As.

Women in Hindu literature; Female Education; Marriage Customs; Widow Marriage; means to be adopted to raise the position of Women.

The above complete in one volume, 1 Rupee Net. Postage, 2½ As.

Prize Essay on the Promotion of Indian Domestic Reform. 8vo. 144 pp. 4 As. Post-free, 5 As.

The prize was gained by Ganpat Lakshman, of Bombay, in 1841. His Essay was published with a Prefatory Note by the Rev. Dr. John Wilson, in which it is highly commended as giving a graphic and correct picture of Hindu family life.

RELIGIOUS REFORM.

(See also The Sacred Books of the East Described and Examined. List on last page of wrapper.)

Popular Hinduism. 8vo. 96 pp. 2½ As. Post-free, 3½ As.

Review of the Hinduism of the Epic Poems and Puranas, &c.; Rites and Observances; Effects of Hinduism, and Suggested Reforms.

PHILOSOPHIC HINDUISM. 8v. 72 pp. 2½ As. Post-free, 3 As.

The Upanishads; the Six Schools of Hindu Philosophy; the Minor Schools; Doctrines of Philosophic Hinduism; the Bhagavad Gita; Causes of the Failure of Hindu Philosophy.

THE BRAHMA SAMAJ, AND OTHER MODERN ECLECTIC RELIGIOUS SYSTEMS. 108 pp. 3 As. Post-free, 4 As.

Modern Hindu Theism; Rammohun Roy; Debendranath Tagore; Keshub Chunder Sen; the Sadharan Brahmo Samaj; Madras Brahmoism; Prarthana Samajes.

INDIA HINDU, AND INDIA CHRISTIAN; OR, WHAT HINDUISM HAS DONE FOR INDIA, AND WHAT CHRISTIANITY WOULD DO FOR IT. 8vo. 72 pp. 2½ As. Post-free, 3 As.

Address to thoughtful Hindus, showing how much their country would benefit from the religion which many of them now oppose.

KRISHNA AS DESCRIBED IN THE PURANAS AND BHAGAVAD GITA. 8vo. 72 pp. 2½ As. Post-free, 3 As.

A full account is given of the Krishna Avatara, chiefly taken from the Vishnu Purana, with some extracts from the Bhagavata Purana and the Mahabharata; the circumstances which led to the great war between the Pandus and Kurus are described; and some of the doctrines of the Bhagavad Gita are examined in detail.

ACCOUNT OF THE TEMPLE OF JAGANNATH AT PURI. 8vo. 48 pp 1½ As.

The account is taken chiefly from Dr. Rajendralala Mitra's *Antiquities of Orissa*; Hunter's *Gazetteer of India*, Sterling's *Orissa*, &c. With views of the temple, procession, and images.

CHRISTIANITY EXPLAINED TO A HINDU; OR, THE DOCTRINES OF CHRISTIANITY AND HINDUISM COMPARED. 60 pp. 2 As.

Doctrines about God, Creation, the Soul, Karma, Transmigration, Sin, Incarnations Salvation, Prospects at Death, and Comparative Effects.

SWAMI VIVEKANANDA ON HINDUISM. 8vo. 96 pp. 3 As. Post-free, 4 As.

The Swami's Chicago Address is quoted in full and examined; important facts are brought out which he omitted to state.

THE HISTORY OF CHRISTIANITY IN INDIA; WITH ITS PROSPECTS. 8vo. 150 pp. 5 As. Post-free, 6 As.

An account of the early Christian Missions, and the progress of Christianity among the principal nations; with 35 illustrations, including portraits of some eminent Missionaries.

TESTIMONIES OF GREAT MEN TO THE BIBLE AND CHRISTIANITY. 8vo. 45 pp. 1½ As. Post-free, 2 As.

Opinions expressed by great writers, philosophers, scientists, lawyers and statesmen, showing that the Bible and Christianity are firmly believed by the most eminent men of the time.

HOW THE PEOPLE OF ANCIENT EUROPE BECAME CHRISTIANS, AND THE FUTURE RELIGION OF INDIA. 8vo. 48 pp. 1½ As. Post-free, 2 As.

An account of the Eastern and Western Aryans; their common origin; resemblances in language and religion; how Christianity was first brought to Europe; the opposition it encountered, and its final success, with the evidence that it will follow a similar course in India.

CIVILIZATION, ANCIENT AND MODERN, COMPARED; WITH REMARKS ON THE STUDY OF SANSKRIT. 8vo. 48 pp. 1½ As. Post-free, 2 As.

Hindu Civilization in the Vedic and Puranic Periods, contrasted with that of modern times. The accounts of the former have been largely taken from Mr. R. C. Dutt's *Civilization in Ancient India*. Long extracts are given from Macaulay's celebrated Minute on Indian Education, showing the greater benefits to be derived from Western knowledge than from the study of Sanskrit and Arabic.

DEVIL-DANCERS, WITCH-FINDERS, RAIN-MAKERS, AND MEDICINE-MEN. 4to. 60 pp. 2½ As. Post-free, 2 As.

A full account of these curious and degrading superstitions, prevalent among backward nations in different parts of the world; with 36 illustrations.

TRANSMIGRATION. 12mo. 19 pp. By Rev. Dr. W. Hooper, 1 Anna.

TRACTS FOR MUHAMMADANS. 12mo. 120 pp. 3 As.

By the Rev. Dr. G. Rouse, M. A. Translated from Bengali. The Integrity of the Gospel; Jesus, or Muhammad? ; The Sinless Prophet; The True Islam; The Koran; Fatiha; The Paraclete, &c., are some of the subjects.

DODDRIDGE'S RISE AND PROGRESS OF RELIGION IN THE SOUL. 12mo. 180 pp. 3 As. Post-free, 4 As.

This is an abridged edition of one of the most useful works on Christianity in the English language.

Pice Papers on Indian Reform, ¼ Anna each.

Some are original; others are abridged from the foregoing for popular use.

1. CAUSES OF INDIAN POVERTY.
2. INDIAN MARRIAGE CUSTOMS.
3. SUPPOSED AND REAL CAUSES OF DISEASE.
4. PATRIOTISM: FALSE AND TRUE.
5. MANAGEMENT OF INFANTS.
6. DEBT, AND HOW TO GET OUT OF IT.
7. THE PURDAH; OR THE SECLUSION OF INDIAN WOMEN.
8. CASTE: ITS ORIGIN AND EFFECTS.
9. ASTROLOGY.
10. WHAT HAS THE BRITISH GOVERNMENT DONE FOR INDIA?
11. WHO WROTE THE VEDAS?
12. MANAVA-DHARMA SASTRA.
13. THE BHAGAVAD GITA.
14. THE SCIENCE OF THE HINDU SASTRAS.
15. FEVERS: THEIR CAUSES, TREATMENT, AND PREVENTION.
16. CHOLERA AND BOWEL COMPLAINTS.
17. ANIMAL WORSHIP.
18. EARLY MARRIAGE; ITS EVILS AND SUGGESTED REFORMS.
19. DUTY TO A WIFE.
20. THE FRUITS OF HINDUISM.
21. INDIAN WIDOWS, AND WHAT SHOULD BE DONE FOR THEM.
22. THE ADVANTAGES OF FEMALE EDUCATION.
23. HINDU AND CHRISTIAN WORSHIP COMPARED.
24. HINDU PILGRIMAGES.
25. CHARITY: FALSE AND TRUE.
26. THE TWO WATCHWORDS—CUSTOM AND PROGRESS.
27. THE VALUE OF PURE WATER.
28. CHARMS, MANTRAS, AND OTHER SUPERSTITIONS.
29. NAUTCHES.
30. IMPORTANCE OF CLEANLINESS.
31. HOW TO HAVE HEALTHY CHILDREN.

32. Causes of Indian Poverty.
33. Indian Marriage Customs.
34. Eclipses.
35. Family Prayer.
36. Giving Abuse.
37. Shraddhas.
38. Karma or Fate.
39. The Fatherhood of God.
40. The Brotherhood of Man.
41. Hindu and Christian Ideals on Piety.
42. Prayaschitta.

Complete in a volume, half bound, gilt title, 1 Re. Postage, 2 As.

Exposures of Theosophy.

The Theosophic Craze: its History; the Great Mahatma Hoax; how Mrs. Besant was Befooled and Deposed; its Revival of Exploded Superstitions of the Middle Ages. 8vo. 96 pp. 3 As. Post-free, 4 As.

A sketch is given of the history of the Society since its commencement; the tricks of Madame Blavatsky are explained; an account is given of the many changes through which Mrs. Besant has passed; the worthlessness of the evidence for the existence of Mahatmas is exposed; with an appeal to educated Hindus.

India, Past and Present. 8vo. 96 pp. 2 As. Post-free, 2½ As.

It is considered whether India would benefit more from Hindu or Western Civilization, from Sanskrit or English; with a Notice of India's Present Needs. Theosophist plans for the improvement of India are examined.

Who is Mrs. Besant? and Why has she come to India? 8vo. 48 pp. 1 An.

A sketch of her life, an account of the numerous changes through she has passed, her plans for the benefit of India; with portraits of herself, Madame Blavatsky, and C. Bradlaugh.

Papers for Thoughtful Hindus.

No. 1. The Relation of Christianity and Hinduism. 8vo. 32 pp. By the Rev. Dr. Krishna Mohun Banerjea, late Sanskrit Examiner to the Calcutta University. ½ Anna.

The remarkable resemblances, in some respects, between ancient Hinduism and Christianity are pointed out.

No. 2. The Supposed and Real Doctrines of Hinduism, as held by Educated Hindus. 8vo. 32 pp. By the Rev. Nehemiah (Nilakanth) Goreh. ½ Anna.

It is shown that the belief of educated Hindus with regard to God, His Attributes, Creation, &c., are not found in the Vedas; but have been derived from Christianity.

No. 3. Moral Courage. 8vo. 32 pp. ½ Anna.

A lecture by the Bishop of Bombay.

No. 4. THE IMPORTANCE OF RELIGION. 8vo. 48 pp. ¾ Anna.
An appeal to the young, by John Foster, author of Essay on *Decision of Character*.

No. 5. CHRISTIANITY, OR—WHAT? 8vo. 16 pp. ¼ Anna. By the Rev. H. Rice.
Christianity is shown to be the only religion which meets the wants of man.

No. 6. THE SENSE OF SIN IN THE LIGHT OF HISTORY. A Lecture by the Rev. F. W. KELLETT, M.A., Madras Christian College. 8vo. 20 pp. ½ Anna.
It is shown that the deeper the sense of sin, the more mature the religious life.

No. 7. BISHOP CALDWELL ON KRISHNA AND THE BHAGAVAD GITA. 8vo. 32 pp. ¾ Anna.
A reprint of Remarks on the late Hon. Sadagopah Charloo's introduction to a Reprint of a Pamphlet entitled, "*Theosophy of the Hindus*;" with a preface by the Rev. J. L. Wyatt.

No. 8. THE DUTIES OF EDUCATED YOUNG MEN TO THEIR COUNTRY. 8vo. 16 pp. ½ Anna.
An address, by the Rev. H. Ballantine, at a Meeting of the Ahmednagar Debating Society. Translated from the Marathi.

No. 9 CHRIST THE FULFILMENT OF HINDUISM. 8vo. 23 pp. ½ Anna.
A lecture by the Rev. F. W. KELLETT, M.A., Madras Christian College.

No. 10. VEDANTISM. 8vo. 21 pp. ½ Anna.
By the Rev. Lal Behari Day, with numerous Sanskrit quotations.

No. 11. THE DEFECTIVENESS OF BRAHMOISM. 8vo. 24 pp. ½ Anna.
A Lecture by the Rev. Lal Behari Day.

No. 12. PRELIMINARY DIALOGUES ON IMPORTANT QUESTIONS IN INDIA. 8vo. 74 pp. 2 As. Post-free, 2½ As.

Descriptions of Countries and Peoples.

PICTORIAL TOUR ROUND INDIA. Imperial 8vo. 116 pp. 6 As. Post-free, 7½ As.
An imaginary tour round India, with visits to Nepal and Cashmere, describing the principal cities and other objects of interest. With 97 woodcuts illustrative of the Himalayas, Calcutta, Benares, Agra, Delhi, Bombay, Madras, &c.

THE PRINCIPAL NATIONS OF INDIA. 8vo. 160 pp. 4 As. Post-free, 5 As.
An account of 42 Nations and Tribes of India, with specimens of some of their languages, and 55 illustrations.

THE NATIVE STATES OF INDIA AND THEIR PRINCES; WITH NOTICES OF SOME IMPORTANT ZEMINDARIS. 4to. 100 pp. 5 As. Post-free, 6 As.
157 States are described, and 32 portraits are given. The little book will help to enable Indians to understand the vast extent of their country, and what is being done for its improvement.

KASI, OR BENARES, The Holy City of the Hindus. Imperial 8vo. 44 pp. 3 As. Post-free, 4 As.
An account of the city; its Sanskrit schools, ghats, temples, and pilgrimages; with 23 illustrations.

THE GREAT TEMPLES OF INDIA, CEYLON, AND BURMA. Imperial 8vo. 104 pp. with 60 illustrations. 6 As. Post-free, 7½ As.

There are pictures and descriptions of some of the most celebrated Hindu, Sikh, Jain, and Buddhist temples; as Puri, Budh-Gaya, Benares, Hurdwar, Gangotri, Ellora, Elephanta, Amritsar, Gwalior, Tanjore, Srirangam, Kandy, Prome, and Mandalay.

BURMA AND THE BURMESE. 4to. 54 pp. 2½ As. Post-free, 3 As.

A description of the manners and customs of the Burmese; an account of their government, religion, and history, with illustrative woodcuts, and portraits of King Theebaw and his Queen.

LANKA AND ITS PEOPLE; OR, A DESCRIPTION OF CEYLON. 4to. 72 pp. 3 As. Post-free, 3½ As.

The account of Lanka given in the Ramayana is first mentioned. Its history, and present condition are then described, with numerous illustrative woodcuts.

TIBET: THE HIGHEST COUNTRY IN THE WORLD. 4to. 2½ As.

An account of the country, its productions, the curious customs of the people, their religions, and supposed living incarnations; with numerous illustrations.

PICTORIAL TOUR ROUND ENGLAND SCOTLAND AND IRELAND. Imperial 8vo. 114 pp. 6 As. Post-free, 7½ As.

Descriptions of the chief places of interest; Public Schools and Universities; Coal Mines and Manufactures; the British Government; Home life; England an example and warning to India. With 104 woodcuts, and coloured engraving of the Queen-Empress.

PICTURES OF CHINA AND ITS PEOPLE. 4to. 56 pp. 2½ As. Post-free, 3 As.

Extent, History; Manners and Customs of the People; Schools, Examinations; Industries; Travelling; language and Literature; Government; Religions; India and China compared; with 64 Illustrations.

JAPAN: THE LAND OF THE RISING SUN. 4to. 68 pp. 2½ As. Post-free, 3 As.

With 49 Illustrations. An interesting description of this beautiful country, and an account of the remarkable changes which have taken place in it.

PICTORIAL TOUR ROUND BIBLE LANDS. Imperial 8vo. 100 pp. 6 As. Post-free, 7½ As.

The principal countries mentioned in the Bible and in ancient history are described as Palestine, Syria, Bombay, Asia Minor, Greece and Italy; with 104 Illustrations.

ARABIA, AND ITS PROPHET. 4to. 64 pp. 2½ As. Post-free, 3 As.

An account of the Arabs; with descriptions of Jeddah, Mecca, Medina; the History of Muhammad and the early Caliphs; the Koran, Muslim Doctrines, Sects, Prayers, Pilgrimage, &c.; with numerous illustrations.

PICTURES OF RUSSIA AND ITS PEOPLES. Imperial 8vo. 83 pp. 5 As. Post-free, 6 As.

A description both of European and Asiatic Russia, including an account of the different races by which they are peopled, their manners and customs, the Government, &c.; with 89 illustrations and maps.

EGYPT: THE LAND OF THE PYRAMIDS. Imperial 8vo. 80 pp. 5 As. Post-free, 6 As.

A description of this interesting country, one of the oldest seats of civilization in the world; its ancient religion, its famous temples and other buildings; the manners and customs of the people, etc.; with numerous illustrations.

THE LAND OF SNOWS; with an account of Missions to Greenland. 4to. 56 pp. 2½ As. Post-free, 3 As.

A description of Greenland, so different from India; giving an account of its people, and the efforts to elevate them; with numerous illustrations.

THE OVERLAND JOURNEY TO ENGLAND. 4to. 72 pp. 3 As.

A description of the principal places passed, with some account of the expense, and directions on arrival in England copiously illustrated.

PICTURES OF WOMEN IN MANY LANDS. Imperial 8vo. 112 pp. 6 As. Post-free, 7½ As.

Descriptions of women, beginning with the most degraded nations of the world, and gradually ascending to the most enlightened; with suggestions, from the review, for Indian women, with 172 illustrations.

Biographies.

STATESMEN OF RECENT TIMES. 8vo. 192 pp. 8 As. Post-free, 9½ As.

Accounts are given of the leading Statesmen in the great countries of the world; as Gladstone, Salisbury, Bismarck and others. Special notice is taken of those interested in India. In all 182 are mentioned, with 122 portraits.

THE GOVERNORS-GENERAL OF INDIA, First Series. By Henry Morris, M. C. S. (retired) 8vo. 145 pp. 4 As. Post-free, 5 As.

Contains sketches of the lives of Warren Hastings, Lord Cornwallis, Sir John Shore, Marquis Wellesley, the Earl of Minto, and the Marquis of Hastings, with portraits. Interesting personal details are given, such as are not usually found in histories.

THE GOVERNORS-GENERAL OF INDIA, Second Series. By the same author, 8vo. 175 pp. 4 As. Post-free, 5 As.

Includes Sketches of Lord Amherst, Lord William Bentinck, Lord Auckland, Lord Ellenborough, Lord Hardinge, and the Marquis of Dalhousie.

The two Series, half bound in cloth, gilt title, 12 As.

SKETCHES OF INDIAN CHRISTIANS; WITH AN INTRODUCTION BY S. SATTHIANADHAN, M.A. 8vo. 268 pp. half cloth with gilt title, 10 As. Post-free, 11½ As.

An account of 42 Indian Protestant Christians; Tamil, Telugu, Canarese, Malayalam, Bengali, Hindustani, Panjabi, Afghan, Gujarati, Marathi, Parsi, and Karen; with several portraits.

ANGLO-INDIAN WORTHIES: By Henry Morris, MADRAS C. S. (Retired.) 8vo. 160 pp. 4 As. Post-free, 5 As. Full cloth, gilt title, 8 As.

Lives of Sir Thomas Munro, Sir John Malcolm, Lord Metcalfe, Mountstuart Elphinstone, James Thomason, Sir Henry Lawrence, Sir James Outram, Sir Donald Macleod, and Sir Bartle Frere, with portraits.

EMINENT FRIENDS OF MAN; OR LIVES OF DISTINGUISHED PHILANTHROPISTS. 8vo. 158 pp. 4 As. Post-free, 5 As. Full cloth, gilt title, 10 As.

Sketches of Howard, Oberlin, Granville Sharp, Clarkson, Wilberforce, Buxton, Pounds, Davies of Devauden, George Moore, Montefiore, Livesey, the Earl of Shaftesbury, and others; with remarks on what might be done in India.

SOME NOTED INDIANS OF MODERN TIMES. 8vo. 164 pp. 4 As. Post-free, 5 As.

Sketches of Indian Religious and Social Reformers, Philanthropists, Scholars, Statesmen, Judges, Journalists, and others; with several portraits.

MARTIN LUTHER, THE GREAT EUROPEAN REFORMER. 8vo. 109 pp. 2½ As. Post-free, 3 As.

The state of religion in Europe in the time of Luther is described; a full account is given of his undaunted efforts to bring about a reformation, the greater need of a similar change in India is shown, and Luther is held up as an example. 15 illustrations.

BABA PADMANJI. An Autobiography. 8vo. 108 pp. 2½ As. Post-free, 3 As.

An interesting account by himself of this popular Marathi author, describing his conversion from Hinduism to Christianity.

PICTURE STORIES OF NOBLE WOMEN. 4to. 50 pp. 2½ As. Post-free, 3 As.

Account of Cornelia, Agrippina, Padmani of Chittore, Lady Jane Grey, Ahaliya Bai, Mrs. Fry, Princess Alice, Miss Carpenter, Maharani Surnomayi, Pandita Ramabai, Miss Nightingale, and Lady Dufferin.

THE QUEEN-EMPRESS OF INDIA AND HER FAMILY. 43 pp. 3 As. Post-free, 3½ As.

Her early life; marriage; widowhood; children; progress in India during her reign; traits of character and lessons from her life. With 27 illustrations, and a colored portrait of the Empress.

SIR HERBERT EDWARDES. By Henry Morris. 8vo. 20 pp. ½ Anna.

He is described as the hero of Multan; the peacemaker among wild Afghan tribes; the true friend of India; the earnest Christian.

Publications for Students.

SELECT CONVOCATION ADDRESSES, delivered to Graduates of the Madras University. 8vo. 231 pp. Stiff covers, 8 As.; Half bound in cloth, 12 As. Full bound in cloth, with gilt title, 1 Re. Post-free.

The volume contains 15 addresses, commencing in 1859, and including several of the most recent. Some of the most distinguished men in South India during the last 30 years took part in the Series. Many very useful hints to young men entering upon the battle of life, in any part of India will be found in the collection.

THE INDIAN STUDENT'S MANUAL. 12mo. 352 pp. 8 As. Post-free, 9 As.

Hints on Studies, Examinations, Moral Conduct, Religious Duties, and Success in Life.

Progress.

This is a monthly illustrated Periodical for the educated classes in India and Ceylon. The subscription is only 8 As. a year; with postage 14 As. Three copies may be sent for ½ anna postage.

The Periodical is specially recommended to TEACHERS. It would give new ideas to their pupils, while the page for students would be very useful to those preparing for examinations.

Orders to be addressed to Mr. A. T. SCOTT, Tract Depôt, MADRAS.

YOGA SASTRA